eBay 102:
What No One Else Will
Tell You About eBay

by Michael Ford

**eBay Power Seller and
seven time author**

Trademarks

Don't Bid On It™, Snipe-To-Win™, and related names are trademarks of Elite Minds Inc. These trademarks may not be used without written permission from Elite Minds Inc. All other trademarks are the property of their respective owners whether designated as trademarks or not.

NEITHER THE PUBLISHER NOR AUTHOR MAKE ANY REPRESENTATIONS OR WARRANTIES WITH RESPECT TO THE ACCURACY OR COMPLETENESS OF THE CONTENTS OF THIS WORK AND SPECIFICALLY DISCLAIM ALL WARRANTIES, INCLUDING WITHOUT LIMITATION WARRANTIES OF FITNESS FOR A PARTICULAR PURPOSE. NO WARRANTY MAY BE CREATED OR EXTENDED BY SALES OR PROMOTIONAL MATERIALS. THE ADVICE AND STRATEGIES IN THIS WORK MAY NOT BE APPROPRIATE OR SUITABLE FOR EVERY SITUATION. THIS WORK IS SOLD WITH THE UNDERSTANDING THAT NEITHER THE PUBLISHER NOR THE AUTHOR ARE ENGAGED IN RENDERING LEGAL, ACCOUNTING, OR OTHER PROFESSIONAL SERVICES. IF PROFESSIONAL ASSISTANCE IS REQUIRED, THE SERVICES OF A COMPETENT PROFESSIONAL PERSON SHOULD BE SOUGHT. NEITHER THE PUBLISHER NOR THE AUTHOR SHALL BE LIABLE FOR DAMAGES ARISING FROM THE USE OF INFORMATION OR ADVICE IN THIS WORK. THE LISTING OF A WEBSITE, GROUP, OR ORGANIZATION IN THIS WORK DOES NOT CONSTITUTE ENDORSEMENT BY THE PUBLISHER OR AUTHOR. INTERNET WEBSITES LISTED IN THIS WORK MAY HAVE CHANGED OR DISAPPEARED SINCE THIS WORK WAS PUBLISHED.

EVERY REASONABLE ATTEMPT HAS BEEN MADE TO VERIFY THE ACCURACY OF THE INFORMATION IN THIS PROGRAM, HOWEVER NEITHER THE AUTHOR, PUBLISHER, NOR ANYONE ASSOCIATED WITH THE PRODUCTION OF THIS WORK ASSUMES ANY RESPONSIBILITY FOR ERRORS, INACCURACIES, OR OMISSIONS. THIS PROGRAM MAY MAKE SUGGESTIONS REGARDING MARKETING, SALES, AND ADVERTISING, WHICH ARE GOVERNED BY STATE LAWS WHICH MAY VARY. CHECK YOUR LOCAL LAWS AND THE RULES AND REGULATIONS OF EBAY. THE EBAY RULES AND REGULATIONS MAY HAVE CHANGED SINCE THIS PROGRAM WAS CREATED. SOME EBAY FEATURES REFERENCED IN THIS PROGRAM MAY HAVE CHANGED OR BEEN REMOVED SINCE THIS PROGRAM WAS PRODUCED.

For copyright reasons, all auctions shown in this program are either created by the author or are simulated auction pages created for the purposes of illustration. The user ID's are fictitious or obscured to maintain the privacy of eBay users. All images were created for this program or are known to be royalty free or public domain images, or were used with permission of the copyright holder.

eBay® is a trademark of eBay Inc. PayPal® is a registered trademark of PayPal Inc. This program was produced independently by Elite Minds Incorporated and is not a product of or endorsed by eBay Inc. or PayPal Inc.

eBay 102: What No One Else Will Tell You About eBay
Previously published as Don't Bid On It First Edition
Published by Elite Minds Inc
355 N Lantana St #562
Camarillo CA 93010

ISBN 0-9845361-2-4
ISBN-13 978-0-9845361-2-2

Manufactured in the USA

For more information, bulk quantities, and other books, visit www.EliteMindsInc.com or www.Dont-Bid-On-It.com

About The Author

Michael Ford began his eBay career in 1998 and first became an eBay Power Seller in 2001. His software business has expanded beyond eBay, but he still enjoys buying and selling on eBay as a collector of antique arcade games. Michael has authored a number of books on antique arcade games, game restoration, and computer security. He is a regular contributor to collector magazines and he is a well known business writer.

Michael has always been an entrepreneur and eBay has helped develop those independent business drives into several full-fledged commercial ventures.

Michael is known for 'telling it like it is' and has a no nonsense approach to business and writing. He focuses on details which led him to document and analyze eBay auctions in a hard hitting way in order to determine what works and what does not. Michael's continued his quest for knowledge by monitoring the unsavory side of eBay which resulted in protection measures that are commonly used to identify fraudulent buyers and sellers.

Michael knows both the good and bad sides of eBay and has shared his experiences and techniques to help eBay members gain the most from eBay without losing their shirt to scammers.

Sometimes life is like a box of chocolates bought on eBay.

QUICK REFERENCE

Buyer Quick Reference

- Compare the Seller's eBay ID, Mailing Address, and email address for inconsistencies
- Research Pricing
- Check Seller Feedback
- Check Seller Sales and Buying History
- Shady Seller Check - Review Description for Warning Signs
- Check Payment Terms
- Check Shipping Terms
- Compare similar auctions
- Decide on a price you will be happy with before placing a bid
- Set your Snipe Bidding software
- Never use an unknown escrow company recommended by the seller
- NEVER CLICK ON AN EMAIL LINK FOR PAYPAL OR EBAY!

Seller Quick Reference

- Compare the Buyer's eBay ID, Mailing Address, and email address for inconsistencies
- Never use an unknown escrow company recommended by the buyer
- Check the buyer's buying history for patterns
- Beware of a buyer who wants to pay in an unusual way
- Beware of a buyer who wants the item shipped to someone else's name
- Beware of a buyer who wants the item shipped to Romania, Indonesia, Nigeria or another known problem country
- Verify PayPal payments before shipping, don't rely on email confirmations
- NEVER CLICK ON AN EMAIL LINK FOR PAYPAL OR EBAY!

Important Links

Auction bidding and selling program tutorials
    http://bonus.DontBidOnIt.com eBay Seller Mastery Course
    http://portal.dont-bid-on-it.com

Free spoof/phishing protection toolbar to protect your eBay and PayPal accounts
    http://www.MyLittleMole.com

Auction Snipe Bidding Software
    http://www.snipe-to-win.com

CONTENTS

Starting A Part/Full-Time eBay Business?

Want To Learn How To Turn eBay Into A Cash Machine?
The **eBay Mastery Course** reveals everything you need to know!
Find out more, go here for a free video course:
http://SeminarBonus.DontBidOnIt.com or get the full course here:

http://Bonus.Dont*Bid*On*It*.com

- Transcript of a two hour seminar on starting your eBay business
- White Paper On Importing From China
- How To Become A Power Seller In 90 Days
- Creating your own information products – Step By Step Guide
- Ten Wholesale and Drop Ship Supplier Lists With How-To Guide
- eBay Consignment guide
- Insider Guide To Real Estate Scams On eBay
- Insider Guide To Vehicle Scams On eBay
- Cashing In On Holidays
- Making Money Selling Magazine Subscriptions
- Buying and Selling Websites on eBay
- Audio version of Don't Bid On It book
- Audio version of Scams and Scoundrels book
- Snipe bidding guide
- Web resources you can use to start your business
- Over 40 eBooks plus other audio books to help you start your own eBay business.

Start and/or grow a business on eBay with this course.
The transcript explains:
- How to find products to sell
- Find what's Hot on eBay
- How to market your eBay business to increase sales
- The truth about eBay Stores
- How to do market research and sales analysis
- Why you have an advantage over existing sellers(or how you can get one.)
- How to find and use Drop Shippers, Wholesalers, Manufacturers and more sources for products

INTRODUCTION

Welcome to the *Insider's Guide To eBay: How To Buy And Sell Like A Pro.* I am thrilled that you chose this program because I love to share my eBay experiences. Since I joined eBay in 1998, I have bought and sold thousands of auctions. As a seller, I learned what works and what does not. As a buyer I learned how to obtain the best price without falling victim to a scam. I hope my advice will help you become a better buyer and seller on eBay and I know I can save you a lot of headaches with the seven keys to avoid being scammed.

This program is for both beginners who have never used eBay and experienced eBay users who have been buying and selling for years. I see both experienced and new members making mistakes that cost them money as buyers and sellers. Everyone will learn something from this program. I call it a program and not a book because it is more than a story or quick reference. This book is part of a complete system that will make your eBay experience much safer and more enjoyable not to mention more profitable. The first part of this program is this book which explains the in's and out's of eBay and PayPal. The additional parts include the *eBay Scams - The secret to trading safely with eBay and Paypal* book which helps you avoid scams, the free software tools at AuctionInquisitor.com and the eBay Mastery Course at http://bonus.dontbidonit.com which contains the secrets carefully guarded by top eBay sellers.

We will discuss PayPal extensively. PayPal is the payment system used on eBay. We could never discuss eBay fully without covering PayPal.

Even if you are already on eBay, I encourage you to go through the beginner and account setup sections. You will find many tips and tricks. This advice will not only improve your eBay experience, it will help protect you from criminals.

As a buyer, you will learn how to determine the amount to bid, how to place the most effective bids that can win, how to obtain the best price and how to pick trustworthy sellers. As a seller, you will learn how to setup auctions that will attract the most interested buyers, how to answer questions before they are asked, how to present a professional and trust inspiring auction listing, how to avoid fraudulent bidders, plus many more tips you will need to be a top notch eBay'er.

Before I continue, I want to stress that I have made thousands of great transactions on eBay. In this program, I highlight some of the bad experiences I have had both to entertain and to show you how to avoid them. Even though I relate my bad experiences, these are in no way examples of the average eBay transaction. These are the exceptions. Out of my tens of thousands of transactions using eBay and PayPal, I have had very few bad experiences. The majority of eBay users are honest people interested in making a legitimate transaction.

You do not have to jump in to the fire all at once. You can and should start small. Buy a few items here and there as you need them. Then sell an item or two that you no longer need. These small transactions will quickly gain you experience and confidence in using eBay. After completing this program, your friends will be coming to you for advice.

Good Luck and **Don't Bid On It**™, until you have finished this program!

CHAPTER 1 - WHAT IS EBAY?

Did you check eBay?

I was looking through eBay last night and you wouldn't believe what I found.

I bought it on eBay.

How many times have you heard statements like these and wondered, *"Why does everyone think eBay is so great?"*

EBay is the world's largest marketplace. EBay does not actually sell anything. It is a website where the average person can offer items for sale. Site visitors can make offers in the form of bids to buy the items. EBay sets up rules and monitors auctions for safety and fairness. It is just like a flea market. Everyone has their own booth and can offer items they want to sell. Fortunately, there is no walking! You can do all of your browsing from the comfort of home.

An item's value is determined by the people who are interested in it. When you walk into a store, everything is marked with a price tag. Wouldn't it be great if you could make an offer for an item instead of paying full price? On eBay you can. It is just like a live auction except it is on the Internet. You make your offer by typing in a bid amount that you are willing to pay for an item. If no one bids higher than your bid before the auction close time, you win the item. The value is determined by what the high bidder is willing to pay. Sometimes the value is high because many people want the item. Sometimes the value is low because no one has noticed the item. It really makes auctions exciting and sometimes results in the winner walking away with a bargain.

Seller *The person with an item they want to sell. They pay a small fee, to list their item for sale.*

Bidder *The person who wants the item and makes an offer in the form of a bid. EBay members can bid on items for sale until the end of the auction. The highest bidder is the auction winner.*

EBay is the ideal place to find a bargain or a rare collectable. If you are a collector or hobbyist, you will find something that interests you on eBay. Even if you are not looking for anything in particular, it is fun to go through the eBay listings and see what other people are offering. You can find anything from replacement Christmas Tree Lights to Cars and even cities have been sold on eBay. You may find a new collectable that interests you; one that you never knew existed before. You may learn something new or re-live nostalgic memories from the old toy auctions.

What do people sell on eBay? Everything! Some people clean out their garages or attics and sell items they no longer use, some buy and sell collectables, some people use eBay as their primary source of income and buy and sell new items on it as a full time business.

EBay is a marketplace where millions of buyers search daily for specific items. It is a seller's dream come true. You have one place where millions of people are actively looking for what you are selling. When someone looks at your eBay auction, they are already interested in buying. They have made the decision that they want the item you have listed. They are just looking for the right seller to buy from. You actually have people lined up wanting to buy your item! Selling has never been so easy.

Main eBay webpage

Why Buy or Sell on eBay?

You may be cautious or even fearful about buying or selling on eBay. Everyone is hesitant to jump into something as big as eBay without understanding it. EBay is not scary at all once you know how it works. Buying an item without seeing it may seem strange at first, but it is no different than buying from a catalog. It is actually fun to browse eBay and really fun to buy something at a bargain price.

You can buy and sell lots of useful things on eBay like
*   Children's clothes
*   Brand name clothes
*   Broken items(sold for parts)
*   Tools
*   That old computer you don't use anymore
*   Last year's video game console which is sitting in the closet
*   Collectables
*   Exercise equipment
*   Books
*   Original Music CD's
*   Original DVD Movies
*   Video Games
*   Electronics
*   Dishes
*   Antiques
*   And much more

What you Can't sell on eBay
*   Counterfeit items(documents, money, clothing, software, movies, music)
*   Illegal items, Infringing items(Copies of CD's, copies of movies or software etc)
*   Prescription Drugs
*   Firearms
*   Human Remains
*   Police Badges

You can offer some items with restrictions like alcohol.

See the eBay policy for more details and a longer list of prohibited items. You can find a shortcut to this list at http://portal.dont-bid-on-it.com

> *Sending a Message Center message with the word 'firearms' or 'police badge' on eBay or PayPal can cause your account to be suspended. It is not a good idea to even discuss prohibited items through the Message Center.*

Junk or Treasure?

One persons junk is truly another's treasure on eBay.

Do you need a new garage door opener? Someday you will and somewhere, someone has exactly what you need and it may be on eBay. An item like an old garage door opener may be impossible to find. EBay is often the only source for hard to find items like these.

There are many items on eBay that are not available anywhere else. Antiques and collectables are a perfect example. You could never go into a retail store and have your pick of 20 original Charlie McCarthy dolls, but on eBay it is a daily occurrence. There are sellers on eBay who specialize in re-selling damaged or returned merchandise. When someone returns merchandise to a store, it is sent to a liquidator to be sold at a discount. These liquidators often have large stocks of perfectly good and tested merchandise with some scratches or in an open box. If you are willing to take an open box or an item with some scratches you can save a lot of money when you buy these items on eBay.

EBay expands your interests. You can find new collectables and even businesses that you never knew about before. I have always loved the tin lithograph toys made in the 1950's. I never considered collecting them because I never saw them anywhere. One day, after I had already been on eBay for years, I decided to search eBay. There were countless listings for these beautiful lithograph toys and the prices were great. I now have a collection of these toys and show them off to every visitor I can. I never could have built my collection so easily or for so little money without eBay.

Items I have purchased through eBay

Yard Sale Anyone?

Why not sell it locally in your newspaper classified ads or a yard sale?

If you sell locally, only a handful of people will ever see you item and then you have to set a price. What if your price is too low? Too high? You may not sell the item or you may sell it for much less than it is worth.

What if your item is a collectable toy robot and there are no toy robot collectors in your area? You may not sell the item even though it is valuable. Even worse, you may sell it for $5 and later find it was worth $500. Now if we put the same item on eBay, there will be thousands if not hundreds of thousands of potential toy robot collectors. You set an opening price and then let others bid what they are willing to pay. Each bidder can outbid the previous bidder. At the end of the auction, usually 7 days, the person who has bid the highest amount will be the winner of your auction. No collector will let a rare toy robot sell for $5 when they can bid $20. When another collector sees a rare robot at $20 they may bid $100. The bidders will keep bidding up the price until it reaches its true market value. Selling through eBay is the best of all worlds. You have collectors actively looking for your item. You receive the highest price because you have bidders competing and you have the largest number of potential buyers seeing your item.

Avoiding Fraud

Fraud is a fact of life today, and well...for the past several thousand years. Fraud on eBay is no different from any other type of fraud. It can be avoided most of the time by taking simple precautions.

I have seen many complaints and sad stories about eBay transactions that went bad. Almost all of them result from a failure to do some basic checking into the seller's history or from failure to use common sense. Many of those who are victims of fraud later say *"I thought it was strange..."* or *"I knew something was not right...then I sent the payment."*

Later, we will cover seven simple techniques that you can use to minimize or eliminate your chance of being the victim of fraud. Our **Scams And Scoundrels** book covers frauds and information on recovering your money in more detail.

The benefits I have gained far outweigh the few inconveniences I have experienced. I check eBay almost every day and I am always watching more than one auction. By following the fraud protection advice in this program, I know I can safely buy and sell on eBay.

Don't Bid On It! Finish this program first!

PART I THE BASICS
CHAPTER 2 - eBAY ACCOUNT SETUP

SETTING UP AN eBAY ACCOUNT

Before you can begin buying or selling on eBay, you will need to create an eBay account. Even if you have an account, I suggest you go through this section. You may learn something…actually, you WILL learn something. Much of the following information applies to both PayPal and eBay. We will discuss PayPal after we setup an eBay account.

Setting up an account is easy. I suggest going to http://portal.dont-bid-on-it.com where you will find an a direct link to the setup page with setup instructions and other useful links to special eBay pages.

EBay asks for some general information so they will know who you are and how to contact you.

CONTACT EMAIL ADDRESS

The first piece of information eBay needs is your email address.

If you use a free email service, like yahoo.com, hotmail.com, or gmail.com, you will be asked for additional information to prove you are who you say you are. You can use the email address from your ISP to avoid this extra check. If you have an @aol.com address, I do not recommend using it.

> *No @aol.com email addresses*
> *Among experienced Internet users, AOL users are generally considered, well... inexperienced. AOL appeals to people who are not Internet savvy and therefore make many Net Etiquette mistakes. Experienced eBay users view people who have AOL accounts as beginners and do not want to conduct business with them. Listing an @aol.com address in an auction can reduce the number of bids it receives. Another reason experienced eBay users dislike @aol.com addresses is the unreliable mail service. I cringe when someone sends me an email from aol.com because I know when I reply there is only a 50/50 chance the person will receive my reply. If their email filters are not setup correctly, they will never receive my response and may assume I did not respond. Do not use an @aol.com email address for your auctions or as your only contact address.*

The email address you give to eBay is mostly private. It will only be shared with members you conduct business with. If you buy or sell an item, it will be available to the other party so they can contact you. Your email address does not appear on your auctions unless you choose to include it. Members who send you messages through the eBay Message Center never see your address and you can select to hide your address when you reply to messages in the Message Center. This allows you to keep your email address private.

ADDRESS AND MAIL DROP SERVICES

EBay requests your physical address. This address is sent to sellers so they know where to ship items you purchased. It can also be shared with buyers who want to send payment by money order.

It is not always wise to openly share your home address. You can rent a private mailbox if you plan to run a business out of your home or if you want to keep your home address private. There are many mailbox companies that will rent you a box and accept mail for you privately. A mailbox service is handy for receiving packages too. They will accept UPS and FedEx packages that require a signature during the day. You can pick up your packages at your convenience without worrying about packages being left on the doorstep.

A Post Office box is also good for receiving payments from buyers. Some buyers may view a post office box as shady and not trust the seller who does not give a physical address. This is why a mail drop service is a better choice. Most buyers will pay using PayPal and will not be concerned about a seller with a PO Box.

You should choose the information you use to register carefully. It may be shared with buyers who need to send you payments by mail and sellers who need to ship your items. It is generally a bad idea to give out your home address to people you do not know. Your sign-up information must be accurate. EBay can cancel your account if they are unable to verify the information. They may email or call to verify the information is correct.

EBᴀʏ ID

EBay identifies members using a unique member ID which is your eBay username.

Your eBay ID cannot be a website address or an email address.

Unacceptable user ID's: yourname@yourisp.com
yourcompany-com

EBay generally does not want people advertising their own websites and has restrictions on using your URL in auction listings or in your user ID. EBay wants everyone to come to their site, not go to your website. EBay no longer allows the use of email addresses as user ID's for privacy reasons.

Most people choose a short nickname for their eBay ID. Do not use your full real name for your user ID. Make sure your ID is not a name you would be embarrassed to reveal. There may be times when you need to give your ID to friends, family, or co-workers.

Using suggestive or inappropriate user ID's makes the user seem untrustworthy or shady. A bad user ID name can reduce your high bid amounts if you sell anything.

Inappropriate Ids

- **I-Scam-You** – don't use names that will make other members distrust you
- **Hotchick69** – don't use inappropriate or potentially embarrassing names
- **Fjkdjakfadkjfkdjfkd** – don't use nonsense names
- **^#*$0!** - don't use odd characters
- **Mixelplik** - avoid confusing names, others may not get the reference
- **FORTHEIRS** - is it Fort Heirs or For-The-IRS
- **boobearlover** is it boo-bear-lover or boob-ear-lover

Make sure your ID makes sense and is not offensive

Combined words should make sense together or separate them with a hyphen. Misunderstood ID's can cost you sales if you are a seller and may even cause cancelled bids if a seller is suspicious of your ID.

An ID may seem really cute or interesting to you, but not to others. Using an ID that seems strange will cause buyers(and sellers) to distrust you.

There are millions of members so all of the short common names were taken long ago. You may have to settle for your desired name plus a series of random numbers. Don't use the year as a number **useridebay2007** and don't use a suggestive number **useridebay69 useridebay666**, those are not appropriate in the eBay environment.. Don't worry about picking the wrong ID. You are not stuck with it for life. You can change your user ID every 30 days.

You cannot use the word 'eBay' in your user ID. It is reserved for eBay employees.

Use a generic ID. There is no reason to reveal that you are a doll head vase collector, vaseheadcollectorebay2001. There may be times when you do not want other buyers or sellers to know you are an experienced collector. Your interests may also change over time. I suggest using a generic name like johns-ebay-stuff24501. Save the creative and self expressive ID's for your World of Warcraft account.

Password

The password is what keeps other people from accessing your account. Everyone can see your user ID, but no one should know your password.

Keep your password secure. Do not write your password down where anyone can find it. Do not pick a password that would be obvious to anyone who knows you. You do not want friends or family to guess your password and access your account. You should never use simple passwords like your name, your pet's name, or a common phrase. It should not be a single word either.

Pick a sentence you can easily remember. Then use the first letter from each word as your password. Add either a number or punctuation to the end or beginning.

My Mother Loves Apple Pies In The Morning!

The password would be mmlapitm! This is a password that no one could guess and it is easy to remember. Adding a number or punctuation to the beginning or end makes it much harder for a hacker to figure out. Simply change it to My Mother Loves Ten Apple Pies In The Morning for a password of mml10apitm. Hackers have known methods to automatically test for common passwords like john1 or john2007 and any dictionary word.

Hint: Don't use either of these passwords! They are well known. Make up your own sentence.

Bad passwords

- mydogspot
- happybirthday
- mike
- mike1
- mike2007

Compromised Passwords

If your password is compromised, it is not an eBay or PayPal problem. The hacker did not obtain your password from eBay or PayPal. They obtained your password from you. It could be from a look-alike website which was linked in an email you received, a trojan program on your computer that captured your password, a friend or family member that knows your password, or your password may have been easy to guess.

If your password is compromised (someone finds out what it is), change it immediately.

It it will cause you lots of problems if you do not quickly change your password to prevent others from accessing your account.

Bad guys can post fake auctions using your account in an attempt to use your good feedback to scam buyers. This is called account hijacking. If the bad guy knows you and wants to attack you personally, they can post false feedback for others members or post auctions that violate eBay policy, and bid on expensive items using your account. They may post fake auctions for expensive items to run up your eBay fees. Avoid all of these problems by keeping your passwords secret.

Identity theft most often occurs with friends and family. The same is true of stolen passwords. Make sure current boyfriends/girlfriends do not know your password. When they become ex's you can avoid a problem and you will be glad you kept your password secure. You should never share your password with anyone including family and friends. No one has any legitimate reason to even ask for your eBay or PayPal password. Your password is for you and you alone.

If you think your password has been compromised, or just suspect someone may know what it is, immediately change it. Don't wait. Don't hope for the best. Login to your account and change it right then.

You may be too late and find the bad guy has changed your password to something new locking you out of your account. If this happens, first try to reset your password using the 'Forgot Password' link. If this is unsuccessful, go to the Live Help section of eBay from their main page and explain what has happened. If your PayPal password has been compromised call their support number or email directly or both. By contacting their security centers you can at least minimize the damage and maybe lock the accounts to prevent the bad guy from using them until everything is straightened out.

> *You can use the Live Help link on the eBay main webpage eBay.com to contact support. EBay uses the live help chat feature instead of phone support because it is much more efficient. Live Help online support saves eBay time and allows their operator to help several people at once.*

EBay and PayPal request that you select a secret question. If you forget your password, they can use the answer to this question to verify that you are who you claim to be. They can then reset your password to a new temporary password.

If you are careful with your passwords and only enter them into the real eBay or PayPal websites, then you should have no security problems with your account. It still pays to protect yourself by limiting the damage a criminal could do if they did gain access to your account. We will talk more about how to protect your account shortly.

USER AGREEMENT

Read through the eBay user agreement. It is important to understand your obligations as a buyer or seller as well as eBay rules. When you place a bid on eBay, it is not an offer to maybe pay if you still want the item at auction close. It is a promise to pay if your bid is the high bid. It does not matter if you change your mind. Once a bid is placed on eBay, you are agreeing to a contract which you are legally bound to honor. When the auction closes, if you are the high bidder, you have agreed to purchase the item at the specified price.

Important features of the User Agreement

- Every transaction is a legal contract. If you bid on it and win, you bought it and you are legally required to pay the seller the agreed money. Bidding is just like signing a sales contract.

- You agree to pay the eBay fees(if you are a seller). There are no fees for buyers.

- If you are selling illegal or prohibited items, eBay can provide your information to law enforcement for investigation.

- EBay does not sell anything. EBay is a place where buyers and sellers meet to exchange goods or services, similar to a swap meet or flea market.

The user agreement is pretty straight forward. Play by the rules and have a good time.

PRIVACY

You should read the privacy agreement. I can summarize the privacy agreement for you, *'nothing is truly private'*. The information you provide to eBay is not truly private except for your financial information. They cannot give out your credit card or bank account numbers. However, your name and address are items buyers and sellers need. EBay will make your buying and browsing history available to law enforcement by request, no court order required. This may seem invasive, but it actually is not. A buyer does need to know a sellers address to send a money order. A seller does need to know a buyers address to ship the goods. If there is a problem and email is not working, or one party wants to confirm the other is legitimate, then they may need the others phone number. This information is published in the phone book and it is nothing intrusive. You may not like the idea that any law enforcement officer can request your buying and browsing history, but personally, it does not bother me at all. What most users do not realize is that anyone can view any other member's buying and selling history under the advanced search page. Buying and selling histories are not secret. If they were secret, there could be underhanded trading. By keeping everything open and transparent, eBay encourages an honest marketplace.

Another random member of eBay cannot request your personal information. If you enter into a transaction with someone, that person can request your personal information which is limited to your name, address, and phone number. If a bidder places a bid on an item, they can request your contact information. EBay will send you an email if the other party requests your information to let you know. This email will contact their contact information too.

Many sellers are offended when a bidder requests their personal information. Make sure you have a good reason for requesting the information and let the seller know why it was requested.

If you suspect someone's account has been hijacked(taken over by a criminal), you can place a bid and then request the seller's personal information to obtain a phone number. Then call the seller and ask them if they are actually offering the item that has drawn your suspicion.

> *Buying and selling histories are not private. EBay runs an open market to show that there is no funny business going on with sales. This is another reason to use a generic name as your User ID and not your full name.*

SELLER ACCOUNT

After you have confirmed your account, you will want to click the **Upgrade to Seller Account** link in your MyEBay page. There is no reason to wait, while you are setting up your account you might as well make it a seller account because once you learn how to use eBay, you will want to both buy and sell.

When you first setup an account you can buy items. In order to sell you have to provide eBay with additional information. This additional information also proves that you are who you say you are. You can skip this part and add this information later when you decide to become a seller.

BANK ACCOUNTS AND CREDIT CARDS

EBay prefers to deduct seller fees from your banking account. EBay has to pay a fee when they charge your credit card, but they do not have to pay this fee when they deduct from your bank account. This saves them money so they always prefer to deduct fees from your bank account. You can specify either method for eBay to charge you any seller fees. Don't worry about those fees now. They are not expensive and are only charged when you offer something for sale. You are not charged anything when setting up your eBay seller account or when bidding.

You must exercise some caution when sharing financial information with anyone. EBay and PayPal both require some basic financial information which identifies the person setting up the account and pays any fees.

The best way to protect yourself in the event someone gains access to your eBay or PayPal account is to use only credit cards and bank accounts that have limited funds.

You can set up a special bank account just for use with eBay and PayPal. This is a secondary account, not your main bank account. You can do this at your local bank by opening a second personal checking or savings account or you can open a savings account online. If you are a good customer or maintain a minimum balance, most banks will allow you to open a no fee account.

Companies such as ING Direct ingdirect.com, Emigrant Direct emigrantdirect.com or other online banks will allow you to setup no-fee savings accounts.
The purpose of this account is to keep your primary account secure and to give you the maximum control over your money.

Crooks cannot access your primary account to withdraw money if it is not associated with your PayPal or eBay account. If you do not have a bank account setup or prefer not to do so, you can use a credit card and not provide a bank account number during your eBay account setup. You can always return to add these options later.
If you are using a credit card to open your PayPal or eBay account, I suggest you use

a special card just for these accounts. This special card is one you open just for your eBay and PayPal use and should not be used for any other purchases. This special card should have a low credit limit. You can open a new, no fee, card with any major credit card company and call them to request a low credit limit and a low daily spending cap on your card. If someone does gain access to your PayPal account, they cannot transfer a large amount of money from your credit card to your PayPal account. This limits what a criminal can do. Prepaid credit cards are not recommended because they often have very high usage fees. Use a regular no-fee low limit card instead of a prepaid card.

If your special card has a $200 credit limit and you use this card only for funding your PayPal account or paying eBay fees, you never have to worry about a criminal accessing more than $200.

You can also request a debit card when you have your bank account setup. You can then use this as your 'credit card' and you will have all of your funding sources in one account which makes it easy to keep track of charges and reduces your exposure to fraud. A debit card attached to your special eBay/PayPal bank account is by far the best option.

FINISHED

The fun begins after you finish entering your information and accept the service terms. EBay will send you an email to the email address you specified. This is to verify the email is working and that you actually control that email address. This email contains a confirmation link. You will need to use this link to confirm your email address and enable your eBay account.

The eBay confirmation email should arrive within minutes. Your email provider may be filtering email or your email address may be incorrect if the confirmation email does not arrive. If you mistyped your email address during registration, you will have to start over with a new user ID.

Once you click the confirmation link to confirm your email is working, you have a new eBay account with a 'new member' icon 🔓 by your user ID. This new member icon lasts for 30 days after your account is setup. The icon tells other members you are new to eBay.

> *You should never click on links in an email, but the eBay confirmation is a special case. If you setup an account and seconds later receive the confirmation email, and this email has specific information like your full name, you can click on the link. This message was expected so we know it is legitimate. There are dishonest people who send look-alike emails that are not actually from eBay or PayPal. We will discuss those in detail later.*

PART I THE BASICS
CHAPTER 3 - PAYPAL ACCOUNT SETUP

PAYPAL PAYMENTS

While we are setting up accounts lets go ahead and setup a PayPal account. If you are buying or selling on eBay you need a PayPal account.

As a buyer, you will want PayPal because it allows instant payments and it has buyer protection features. As a seller, you will want to offer PayPal because buyers trust sellers who accept PayPal. Buyers also prefer to pay by PayPal because it is so easy.

PayPal is a company that is owned by EBay Inc. PayPal allows anyone with an email address to send money to anyone else using their email address. It is a very secure system and lets the person sending money control how much is sent. PayPal has both buyer and seller protection features. The amounts and terms are limited so make sure you read the PayPal user agreement and refund policy. You can review the current terms on their website.

When you send someone a payment by PayPal, you specify who it goes to and how much is sent. If you share your credit card information with a stranger, they may charge any amount to your card. You have no control over how they use the number. This cannot happen with PayPal because you have full control over the money being sent. If you choose to PayPal $20 to a seller, then $20 is all they can receive.

PayPal account page showing current balance and recent transactions.

23

You can file for a refund if you have paid using PayPal and the seller does not ship your item. If you are a seller and a buyer tries to defraud you by keeping the merchandise and filing for a refund, you can prove delivery and avoid a lot trouble all because you used PayPal

It is no wonder PayPal has become the number one payment method for auctions. It is fast, easy, and secure, plus it is built into eBay's checkout system. PayPal is a great way to buy other items on the Internet. You never have to give your credit card number to companies you are not familiar with if they accept PayPal.

Having a PayPal account adds legitimacy to your auction listings as a seller. Not offering PayPal makes the seller look like a fly-by-night operation. PayPal is THE way people pay on eBay.

PAYPAL ACCOUNT SETUP

To setup your PayPal account I recommend you go to
http://portal.dont-bid-on-it.com
where you will find a PayPal sign-up link along with the latest updated information.

You should use the special secondary bank account previously discussed for the eBay account setup. This limits the possible damage a criminal can do if your PayPal account password should be compromised. Criminals would never be able to access more than the amount in your special secondary account.

You can select personal or business accounts when you setup your PayPal account. The personal account has limits on the amount of money that can be transferred out and personal accounts cannot accept credit card payments. Personal PayPal accounts are also not allowed to be used for eBay payments. Select the Business or Premiere account even if it is for your personal use. These accounts do charge a small percentage (thirty cents plus 2.9%) for each transaction received. If you are a buyer only, this will not affect you. If you are a seller and you make many sales, your shipping and handling fees should easily cover this small PayPal transaction fee. There is no fee for sending money if you are a buyer.

Choosing a business account gives your customers the option of paying by credit card through PayPal even if they do not have a PayPal account.

You should verify your PayPal account by clicking the Verify button in your account page. This gives additional confidence to buyers and sellers who do business with you. A verified account shows that you are who you say you are. Verified accounts have more protection from PayPal. You will have more buyer and seller protection when you verify your Business or Premiere account.

Click on the Verify link on the left side of your account page. PayPal will request some additional information to verify who you are. Once you have provided the information, your account will be marked as Verified and every payment you send will indicate to the seller that you are a Verified PayPal member.

PayPal Requirements for their $5,000 seller protection plan(eBay purchases only)

1. *You must have a Verified Business or Verified Premier Account*
2. *The transaction must be between a US, UK or Canadian parties*
3. *The payment must be a "Seller Protection Policy Eligible" sale on the "Transaction Details" page,*
4. *The payment must be a single payment*
5. *There can be no surcharge for accepting PayPal*
6. *The purchased item must be shipped to the Confirmed Address listed on the "Transaction Details" page*
7. *The item must be shipped within seven days of receiving payment*
8. *You must have trackable online proof of delivery**
9. *You must respond to PayPal's requests for information*

*If the transaction is over $250.00 you must have signature confirmation or other proof of delivery.

PayPal's Buyer Protection Requirements(for eBay purchases)

1. *This is a best effort policy*
2. *Buyers are covered up to $2000.00(there are restrictions and limits)*

You will also want to use your credit card to confirm your shipping address. Click the Confirm Address link in your account page. Many sellers   will only ship to a Confirmed Shipping Address because it offers the most confidence that the account is legitimate. Sellers also have more protection from fraud when they ship to a confirmed address.

You can find more details on PayPal's website. This policy may change or be updated at anytime. The coverage amount is based on a Tier system and may be as low as $200 per purchase depending on the item and circumstances. Vehicles and Live Auction sales are not covered.

Read the PayPal policy before filing a complaint to refresh your memory. Most complaints result from members not reading the policy and assuming they have the maximum coverage on every transaction. Read the terms.

> *PayPal Balance*
> *Keep only enough money in your account to pay for items you want to purchase. Don't let too much money accumulate if you are a seller. If you are doing a lot of business and receiving thousands of dollars a day, you can request that PayPal sweep funds into your bank account automatically and daily. If your account is compromised, this limits the amount that can be lost. If your account is frozen, this limits the money that is tied up until the matter is resolved.*

PAYPAL PASSWORDS

The same password rules apply to PayPal and eBay. You should never share this password with anyone ever. It is for you and you alone.

Do not use the same password on eBay and PayPal. Many hackers depend on this when they send fake eBay look-alike emails. They want to obtain your eBay password and email address so they can login to your PayPal account. Use a different password for eBay and PayPal.

PAYPAL DEBIT CARD

After you have been a member of PayPal for 60 days, you can apply for the PayPal Mastercard Debit card. This debit card will automatically take money out of your PayPal account when you use it like a credit card. You can receive 1% cash back(see the PayPal website for details) when you use the card as a credit card. This cash back offsets some of the 2.9% fee you are charged when you receive money. You can also reduce the 2.9% fee if you are a receiving $3000 or more per month. If you are doing this much business, apply for a 1.9% merchant rate by filling out a form on the PayPal website.

Using the PayPal MasterCard and applying for the merchant rate can effectively reduce your PayPal fees to 0.9% (2.9% - 1% for MasterCard - 1% for merchant rate = 0.9%).

PART I THE BASICS
CHAPTER 4 - EBAY BASICS

BASICS OF EBAY

Let's take a look at the eBay website and see how it works.

We can go to the main page of eBay by typing www.eBay.com into our browser.

The main page of eBay has shortcuts to all of the major features. Auctions are divided into categories to make finding items you are interested in easy. You can search for keywords which is faster than browsing categories if you are looking for something specific. At the very top of the page are links to the most used features. You can find more links at the bottom of the page.

EBay will ask you to sign in using your user ID and password to access some pages like your MyEBay page. You can select the '*keep me signed in*' option if you are the only user of your computer. You will not have to re-enter your password for the rest of the day. If you want to let someone else use your computer, simply click the Sign Out link. Then no one will be able to access your account without the password.

Make sure you only enter your password on the real eBay website which shows the security lock and starts with https:// with the S for Secure site and not http:// without the S

My EBay

You can track your purchases on you're MyEBay page. Here you can see a list of items you recently purchased and their status. You can see if you forgot to pay for something or see if you need to leave feedback for someone.

Auctions are only listed for 30 days so make sure you have paid, received the item and left feedback within that time. You can still access the auctions up to 90 days. Look in your email for the auction number. On eBay, search for this number and it will take you to the auction listing until it is removed 90 days after close. PayPal will keep the auction number and buyer information much longer if the auction has been paid through PayPal. You can use PayPal's advanced search to find the auction by buyer name, email, or auction number.

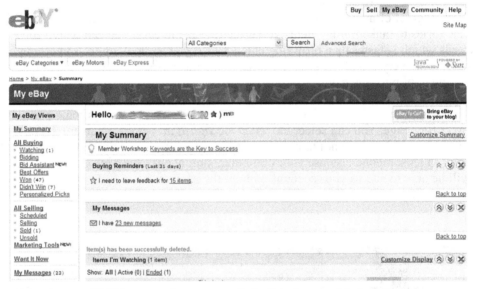

MyEBay page where you can find a list of won and lost auctions, items being watched, account settings, and more

Watched Auctions

This area tracks auctions you are interested in. Every auction has a button that says *'watch this auction'*. When you click this button, the auction is added to your MyEBay page under the Watched Auction section. You can watch auctions you are thinking about bidding on or just interested in keeping an eye on.

You may want to watch an auction without bidding. I often see an item I already have and I want to know what it sells for at the auction close. I may be interested in an item, but not enough to place a bid. Sometimes I am curious to see if an outrageously priced item even sells.

Click the Watch This Auction button in any auction and it will appear in the Watched Auction area of My Ebay(above).

My Ebay shows auctions recently won. You can also click the drop down menu to pay for an auction, leave feedback, contact the seller, or other options.

FAVORITE SEARCHES

I find favorite searches to be the most useful of the favorite features. When you conduct a search, you will see a link beside the results that says '*save this search*'. You can click this link to save this search in your favorites section of your MyEBay page. Every night you will receive an email with the latest search results. If you are looking for an Eldon Bowl-O-Matic vintage bowling game and you save a favorite search for that term, every night you will receive a summary of all auctions with those keywords. You can find items without searching eBay every day. EBay tells you when they are listed. If you search within a category then your search is remembered only for that category. If you search all of eBay, then all of eBay is searched every day for you.

FAVORITE SELLERS

If you are a collector and you find a seller who sells items you are interested in, you may want to know when this seller posts new items. There is a link in the seller's auction that says "Add to Favorite Sellers" Click this link to add the seller to your Favorite Sellers List on your MyEBay page. When the seller posts new items to eBay, you will receive an email notifying you about the new listings. This is a great way to avoid missing auctions you may be interested in and you can scoop up Buy-It-Now auctions before others have a chance to find them.

Favorite Categories

Just like Favorite Sellers, you can pick Favorite Categories. You are limited to four categories so pick carefully. When you select these favorites, you can choose to receive an email when new items are listed. These emails are only sent once per day. You may miss items in active groups if you wait on the email. I check my favorite groups throughout the day and do not rely on this email.
You can select your Favorite Categories on your MyEBay page by selecting Favorites and Categories, then selecting the category you want to add.

EBay Help

You can find answers for almost any eBay question in the eBay Help section. This link is available at the top of every eBay page. If you need to find a specific page perhaps to file a non paying bidder notice and do not know where to look, simply search the help section or use the shortcut link at http://www.dont-bid-on-it.com

About Me Page

EBay has a feature called the 'about me' page. When you create an About Me page, a new icon appears by your user ID which makes you stand out from other sellers who do not have this icon. Even if bidders do not know what it means it will make your ID look special. The About Me page gives you a chance to connect with potential bidders and build trust. You can give the history of your business, you can link to your company website, and you can list your return policy here. In your auction you can always encourage people to visit your About Me page by adding a link "See my About Me page for return policy and payment information" EBay does not allow just any link in an auction, but they will allow links to your about me page in the auction.
It is a very good idea to put any lengthy return or guarantee policy here and link to it from your auction. This keeps your auction listing clean while still making all of the information available.

You should always have a return policy spelled out in your About Me page.

> What to include in your About Me page
> * Link to your business website
> * Link to your eBay store
> * Your return and payment policy
> * Your feedback policy
> * Reference to your other auctions
> * Company history or personal statement about your eBay auctions

This page is public. Don't put anything on your AboutMe page that you would not want a criminal to see.

Live Auctions

A Live Auction is not actually on eBay. It is a real live auction with an auctioneer. When you place a bid on a live auction through eBay you are actually placing an absentee bid at the live auction. When bidding commences, a member of the auction company will bid on your behalf up to your maximum bid.

Live auctions frequently do not disclose shipping until after the auction is closed. You may find you have bought a small $100 vase and been charged $90 in packing and shipping fees. You may bid $1000 for a table and be charged $500 shipping. The amounts listed for live auction opening bids are frequently greatly inflated on eBay. Live auction companies use eBay to draw out those willing to make high bids. The actual item may sell for much less than the opening bid shown on the eBay listing if there are no eBay absentee bidders. It is not uncommon for an eBay listing for a Live Auction item to have an opening bid of $10,000, but at the actual auction, the opening bid may be $3000 and the item may sell for $5,000. EBay bidders are locked out of this auction unless they are willing to spend many times the value of the item. Only the people attending the live auction can bid the lower amounts. The eBay bidder has no way to tap into that low price because the eBay Live Auction prices are inflated by Live Auction listers.

You can find some unusual and rare items in live auction listings. They are great to look through even if you are not a buyer. In Live Auctions you will find rare pieces of art, sculptures by people whose name you recognize, historically significant collectables and more.

Adult Auctions

EBay has a special area for adult users. This area is really for adults, like the back room of the video store. You do not have to worry about accidentally clicking the wrong link and finding yourself in this area. The adult area is separate from all other auctions and you must re-enter your user ID and agree to certain terms to access the adult part of eBay. There may still be racy items in the main listings, but nothing truly adult in nature. Those items are only allowed in the adult section.

EBay Pulse

What are the hot search terms? Biggest seller stores? You can find out in the special Pulse section of ebay at http://pulse.ebay.com/

EBay Shop

I know I said eBay does not sell anything and that is true for the private party auctions listed on eBay. EBay does sell eBay stuff, eBay mugs, beach towels, and novelties in their own EBay Shop. You can find the shop link at the bottom of the main eBay page.

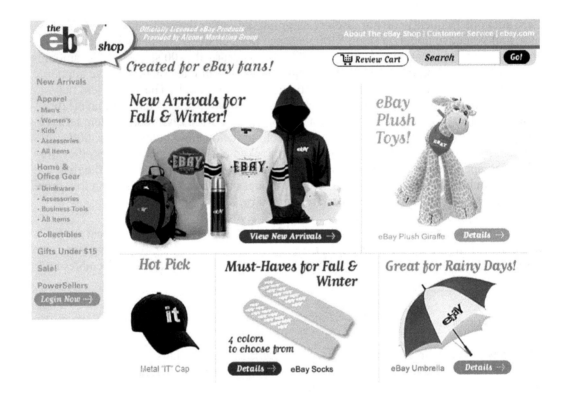

The eBay shop sells shirts, mugs, and other items with the eBay logo.

Community Forums

EBay has a special Community section which is linked from the top of the main page. In the community area you can meet other members who share your interests and ask questions about eBay policies. They offer both message boards and live chat. You can find information on collectables in the eBay category specific forums under the Community link. Many members are happy to answer questions from fellow collectors.

HOT ITEMS

Don't be left out of the hottest trends. See which items are the biggest sellers in each category. EBay keeps a list of hot items in the Seller Central area. You can find Seller Central by clicking the Sell, button at the top of any eBay page and then looking for Seller Central at the bottom of the page. Then click the What's Hot and then Hot Items by Category link to see a list.

EBAY STORES

EBay sellers can create special listings called Stores. These listings look and work just like regular eBay auctions as far as the buyer is concerned. EBay stores are not searched with a regular search unless there are under 30 matches returned for the search terms. You can search eBay stores at eBaystores.com. Store owner's current auctions are also listed in their stores when you search. You can find items in eBay stores that may not show up with a regular search. This area is well worth checking especially if you want a Buy-It-Now option.

An eBay store looks and works the same as an auction with a Buy-It-Now option.

CHARITY AUCTIONS

Charity auctions are used to raise money for established charities. The money raised goes to the charity. Needless to say, this is not the place to look for a bargain. Many people gladly overbid. People seem to find it easier to give to a charity if they receive a token item for their donation. This leads many people to bid high amounts for charity items.

PART II BUYING
CHAPTER 5 - SEARCHING

ADVANCED SEARCH TECHNIQUES

The search feature helps you find specific items, but it can also keep some items hidden. Misspellings or poorly chosen keywords can prevent items from appearing in keyword searches. Such items can be bargains if no other collectors find them.

Keep keyword searches simple. Use as few keywords as possible. If you have too many results you can add keywords to narrow the listings. If you are interested in Arabic language manuscripts, start off by searching for 'manuscripts'. If you receive too many results try 'arabic manuscripts' and try variations that sellers may use like 'middle eastern manuscript' or 'persian manuscript' or 'arabic writing' or 'arabic scroll'. You may even want to search for 'Hebrew manuscript' because a seller may not know the difference if they are not well versed in the language.

TYPO'S

Search for silly typos. Many sellers may make common typographical errors that prevent their items being easily found. Instead of searching for DKNY, search for DNKY, instead of searching for Porsche, try Porshe. Try searching on 'Ralph Luaren' instead of 'Ralph Lauren'. The auctions you find with these typos are seen by fewer people than the auctions with correct spellings so you may find a bargain no one else has bid on.

SEARCH TITLE AND BODY

When you search by keyword, eBay looks at the item title only. Some sellers may not include all of the important keywords in the title or you may be searching for something very specific that would only be listed in the auction description and not in the title.

If you see too many general results using only a couple of keywords, try expanding the search to include the auction title and description and add more keywords. You can check the "*Search Title And Description*" box just under the search box to search both titles and listing text for keywords. By default, eBay searches the titles only.

Advanced Searches

The advanced search panel on the left side of the search or category screen has many options that can help you narrow down results to find exactly the items you are looking for.

You can click the Advanced Search link by the search button to find more advanced search features.

Here you can search to find the items a particular bidder has bid on, what items a seller is selling or has sold, and specific member searches.

Searching For Items

There are two ways to find items on eBay, by looking in categories, which is similar to looking through a catalog, or a keyword search. I am going to start with a keyword search. Keyword searches are the most common way to find specific items. Look through categories when you are interested in a particular type of product, use keyword searches to find specific items.

When using keyword searches, you can search all of eBay or search within a category. This makes it easy to find specific items in a category without a flood of unrelated listings popping up.

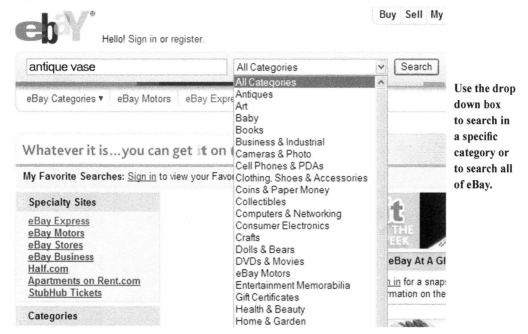

Use the drop down box to search in a specific category or to search all of eBay.

You can find the search box at the top of every eBay page. Simply type in the keywords you are interested in and click the search button to search all of eBay.

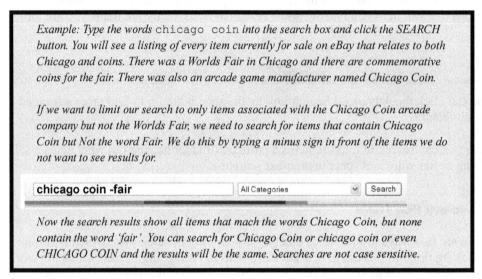

Example: Type the words chicago coin *into the search box and click the SEARCH button. You will see a listing of every item currently for sale on eBay that relates to both Chicago and coins. There was a Worlds Fair in Chicago and there are commemorative coins for the fair. There was also an arcade game manufacturer named Chicago Coin.*

If we want to limit our search to only items associated with the Chicago Coin arcade company but not the Worlds Fair, we need to search for items that contain Chicago Coin but Not the word Fair. We do this by typing a minus sign in front of the items we do not want to see results for.

chicago coin -fair | All Categories ⌄ | | Search |

Now the search results show all items that mach the words Chicago Coin, but none contain the word 'fair'. You can search for Chicago Coin or chicago coin or even CHICAGO COIN and the results will be the same. Searches are not case sensitive.

There are several fancy search options available. You can find a listing of these in the eBay help section. The only one I ever use is the minus sign or NOT operator. It is the most useful operator.

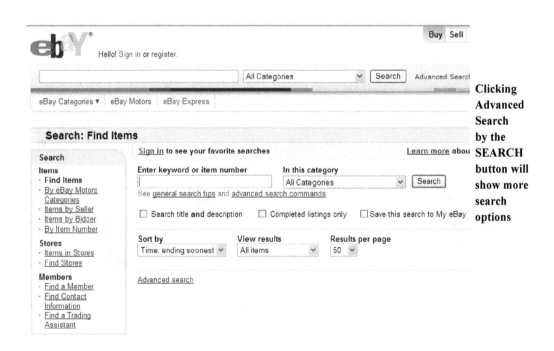

Clicking Advanced Search by the SEARCH button will show more search options

PART II BUYING
CHAPTER 6 - AUCTION ANATOMY

AUCTION LAYOUT

All auctions have the same basic format. At the top we find the important information about the auction, such as price and high bidder. To the right we find information about the seller. Below is the item description. At the bottom of the listing is the shipping and payment information. Let's take a closer look at the information.

- Current Bid – This is the current high bid price. When another bidder places a bid, this will change.

- Buy-It-Now Price – If the seller has selected a Buy-It-Now price, anyone can click this option to buy at a fixed price without waiting until the end of the auction.

- Quantity – This is the number of items available. The Current Bid is the amount for one of these. Most auctions are for only one item or one lot. Some sellers may have cases of goods to sell and offer more than one item.

- End Time – This shows the ending time and the time remaining until the end of the auction. Most auctions last 7 days.

- History – This is the number of bids placed on this auction. More bids mean more people are interested in the auction. Fewer bids may mean no interest, or only experienced bidders are watching the auction and will wait until the final seconds to bid. Few bids can mean the auction was recently listed and no one has had time to see it yet.

- High Bidder- This is the user ID of the person who made the high bid. If there are no bids yet, this will not show up. If the item is a high value item, this may show Bidder_1 instead of a real user ID to protect the user's privacy.

- Item Location – This is the location the item will ship from. This can be important if you want to pick-up the item instead of have it shipped. Some sellers do not allow pick-up of small items so ask first.

- Watch This Item button – This, button adds the item to your Watched Auctions list in your MyEBay page.

- Seller ID – This is the ID of the person selling the item.

- Seller Feedback – Next to the Seller ID is their feedback rating. This is the number of members who have given a positive rating to this member indicating they had a good experience with them.

- Seller Feedback Percentage – The feedback percentage is a percentage of good versus bad feedback. A good seller should have above 98% positive feedback. If a seller is new and only has one negative feedback with 20 positive feedbacks, this percentage may be lower. Most sellers should have a large number of positive feedbacks built up.

- Read Feedback Comments – This shows the comments others have left for the seller. It is the same page seen when clicking on the number rating. Here you can see what other buyers and sellers have said about this member. Look over these and see if the seller has only been a buyer or if they have been buying and selling a long time. If the seller has any negative comments, see what they are and decide if you want to do business with this person or not.

- Member Since – This tells you how long the seller has been on eBay. Sellers offering expensive items who are new members should be regarded with suspicion. A long history and a good feedback rating usually indicate a trustworthy seller. If the sellers account has been hijacked by a criminal this may not be the case. We will cover more on this topic later.

- Ask Seller A Question – click this link to ask the seller a question about the auction. You should read the auction fully before using this link.

- View Seller's Other Items – This link shows all auctions the seller is currently offering. If you are interested in one item, you may be interested in similar items from the same seller.

- Add to Favorite Sellers – This link will add the seller to your Favorite Sellers list in your MyEBay page. When the seller posts new items for sale, you will receive an email notifying you about the new items.

Auction Anatomy 101

Buy-It-Now Price – If the seller has selected a Buy-It-Now price, anyone can click this option to buy at a fixed price without waiting until the end of the auction.

Current Bid – This is the current high bid price. When another bidder places a bid, this will change.

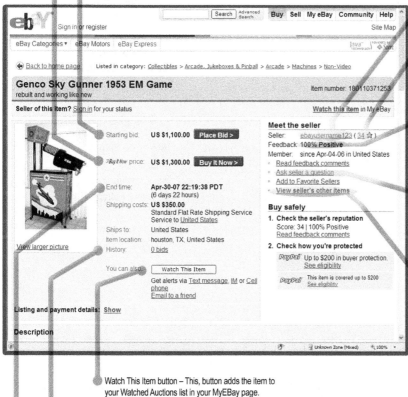

Seller ID – This is the ID of the seller.

Seller Feedback – Next to the Seller ID is their feedback rating. This is the number of good transactions minus the number of bad transactions.

Seller Feedback Percentage – The feedback percentage is a percentage of good versus bad feedback.

Ask Seller A Question – click this link to ask the seller a question about the auction. You should read the auction fully before using this link.

View Seller's Other Items – This link shows all auctions the seller is currently offering. If you are interested in one item, you may be interested in similar items from the same seller.

Watch This Item button – This, button adds the item to your Watched Auctions list in your MyEBay page.

History – This is the number of bids placed on this auction.

End Time – This shows the ending time and the time remaining until the end of the auction. Most auctions last 7 days.

Listing and payment details: Show

Description

This is a 1963 Sky Gunner Electric Mechanical Game made by Genco. It has been fully reworked and repaired. It is in excellent condition. The glass is in very good condition with some flaking as shown in the photos. Feel free to contact me if you have any questions.

Shipping - Local Pickup or I can ship anywhere in the 48 states for $360.00

Payments: PayPal, check, money order

Shipping and handling

Ships to
United States

Shipping and Handling	To	Service
US $350.00	United States	Standard Flat Rate Shipping Service

Country: United States

Shipping and Handling	To	Service
US $350.00	United States	Standard Flat Rate Shipping Service

Shipping insurance
Not offered

Return policy

Return policy not specified.
Read item description for any reference to return policy.

Payment details

Payment method	Preferred/Accepted	Buyer protection on eBay
PayPal VISA AMEX DISCVR e-check	Accepted	*PayPal* Up to $200 in buyer protection. See eligibility. *PayPal* This item is covered up to $200 See eligibility.
Money order/Cashiers check	Accepted	Not Available Not Available
Personal check	Accepted	Not Available Not Available

Learn about payment methods

Take action on this item   Help

Item title: **used**

Place a bid		Buy It Now
Starting bid: **US $1,100.00**		*Buy It Now* price: **US $1,300.00**
Your maximum bid: US $ _____		[Buy It Now >]
(Enter US $1,100.00 or more)		You will confirm in the next step.
[Place Bid >]	or	
You will confirm in the next step		
eBay automatically bids on your behalf up to your maximum bid. Learn about bidding		Purchase this item now without bidding. Learn about Buy It Now

You can also [Watch This Item]

Below the header information is the main description of the item. This is where the seller describes the item being sold. Below the description are the photos.

The shipping details are just below the description.

Below the Shipping Information, you will find the sellers Return policy and payment options

Towards the very bottom you can bid on the auction by entering your maximum bid and clicking the bid, button. Auctions with Buy-It-Now options can be purchased by clicking the Buy-It-Now Button

PART II BUYING

CHAPTER 7 - HOW BIDDING WORKS

LET'S BID!

Wait! **Don't Bid On It!** Not yet. We need to see how this bidding thing works first.

When you place a bid, you are agreeing to buy the item if you should be the high bidder. You have promised to pay the high bid amount if you win. If another member bids more than your bid, you will receive an email notification saying you were outbid and you can then bid more or give up.

EBay uses a bidding system called **proxy bidding**. Proxy bidding means you put in the maximum amount you are willing to bid and eBay will automatically bid for you up to that amount. By using proxy bidding, you do not have to pay the maximum amount you bid unless other members bid up the price.

Here is an example of proxy bidding. Suppose we have an auction that has an opening bid of $1 and no other bidders. The first bidder, Bidder_1, places a bid for $10. This makes the current bid price $1 because this person has met the minimum opening bid of $1. Another bidder, Bidder_2, comes along and bids $5. This is less than Bidder_1's bid so eBay bids on behalf of Bidder_1 up to their maximum $10 bid. There is a minimum bid amount, or a minimum you can go up. You must bid a minimum amount which is a percentage of the price. Ebay shows this amount on the auction so you never have to calculate it. For simplicity, we will use a minimum bid increment of $1.50 in our example. When $5 is bid by Bidder_2, there is already a proxy bid that was placed before this bid for a higher amount. EBay now bids for Bidder_1 using their $10 maximum to outbid the current bidder by placing an automatic $6.50 bid ($5.00 high bid from Bidder_2 plus $1.50 minimum increment). Bidder_2 has now been automatically outbid by a proxy bid of Bidder_1.

Buying consists of these steps

1. Search for an item
2. Research the price
3. Research the seller
4. Place your bid

The $5 bidder will receive a notice immediately saying they were outbid and the current bid is $6.50. Bidder_2 can re-bid a higher amount or quit. In our example this bidder quits. Another bidder comes along, Bidder_3, and bids $30.01 seconds before the auction closes. The current bid is $6.50 but the first bidder already has a proxy bid of $10. In order to top this bid the current bidder must bid more than the highest proxy bid which she did. The new high bid becomes $11.50 (the $10 bid from Bidder_1 who was the high bidder plus the $1.50 minimum bid increment) and the first bidder is emailed a notice saying they were outbid. Our Bidder_3 is now the high bidder at $11.50. If another bidder bids a higher amount before the auction closes, they will have to bid more than $30.01 to win. If they bid less than $30.01, Bidder_3 will pay more for the auction, but will still be the high bidder. In our example, there are no more bids and the auction closes with our Bidder_3 winning the item for $11.50.

To sum all of this up, the bid amount is the second highest bidder's maximum bid plus the minimum bid increment.

Proxy bids are only known to eBay. Other members do not know what they are unless the amount is outbid. Other members only see the current bid, not the maximum proxy amount. Proxy bids allow users to privately place a maximum bid and eBay will bid on their behalf up to that amount.

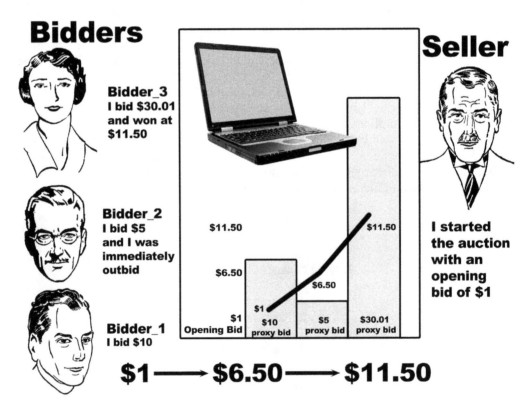

Bidders

Bidder_3
I bid $30.01 and won at $11.50

Bidder_2
I bid $5 and I was immediately outbid

Bidder_1
I bid $10

Seller

I started the auction with an opening bid of $1

$11.50

$6.50

$1 Opening Bid

$1 $10 proxy bid

$5 proxy bid

$6.50

$11.50

$30.01 proxy bid

$1 ⟶ $6.50 ⟶ $11.50

Maximum Bids

Amateur bidders often bid the minimum bid amount because they do not understand proxy bidding. This is a sure way to lose an auction. Never bid the minimum if you want to win. If the opening bid is $10, then bidding $10 or $12 may make you the high bidder for the moment, but it will ultimately lose the auction. Someone will come along and outbid you. Bidding more does not mean you are automatically paying more. Placing a higher proxy bid allows eBay to bid for you up to your maximum. If you bid $30 and no other bidders bid on this $10 auction, then the only bidder who put in a $30 bid will win for $10. If another bidder bids $10.50, they will be automatically outbid by the $30.00 proxy bid making the new bid $12.00. The new bidder may or may not decide to continue increasing their bid.

Bid the maximum amount you are willing to pay and let that run until the end of the auction. Decide what the item is worth to you and bid that amount. Do not keep returning to bid a few dollars more each time. Put in what you are willing to pay and leave the auction alone. If you are outbid, look for another auction and try bidding on it. Returning to re-bid just to be high bidder will result in paying more than the item is worth or more than you can afford. Repeatedly re-bidding just above the minimum is a bad bidding practice and leads to overpaying for an item.

New members on eBay frequently complain that they place a bid and are always outbid. This happens because they are bidding the wrong way. They are bidding too low and too early. They bid below an item's realistic value. No one can expect to bid $30 on a laptop computer worth $500 and win it. They also bid too early which gives other inexperienced bidders an opportunity to bid up the price. Some members give up bidding after they lose a few auctions. Losing is not enjoyable. This is unfortunate because they are so close to winning, but do not realize it. Successful bidding requires placing the right bid at the right time.

Now that you know how proxy bidding works and to bid your maximum bid, I will say **don't do it**. There is a better way. Placing your maximum bid and '*hoping for the best*' is a poor strategy. A better option is to use snipe bidding software to place your bid. I do not recommend proxy bidding at all. Snipe Bidding is discussed in Bidding Strategies.

Practice bidding on live auctions is frowned upon. EBay has setup a special area where you can safely practice bidding without actually bidding on real items.
Go to the eBay Help section and search for 'proxy bidding'. The first item should be the explanation of proxy bidding. Click the first option and click 'test bidding' Here you can enter test bids with no worries about doing anything wrong.

If you bid on a real auction, make sure it is something you are willing to pay for if you win. You should have no problems finding $1 opening bids on expensive items which are safe to bid $1 on. You will be quickly outbid by other bidders. This will gain you experience and confidence in bidding while not costing you any money. Remember, when you place a bid, you are agreeing to buy at that price if you should be high bidder. You are making a legal contract when you bid.

Auctions have a minimum bid amount. You cannot bid one cent above the current price to become high bidder. You must bid the minimum bid amount or higher. This amount is shown in the auction.

If the auction price is $5, you can't win by bidding $5.01, eBay will reject the bid. The minimum bid increase is a percentage of the price. EBay tells you what the minimum bid amount is. You can still use snipe bidding to win an auction for one cent above another bidder and I have done it a number of times. For example, an auction is $0.99 and a bidder bids $5.00 as a proxy bid. This makes the current bid $0.99. I then put in my bid of $5.01 which is above the $0.99 current bid and the $2.04 minimum bid. I am now high bidder because my bid was higher than the first bidder's proxy bid and my bid amount was above the minimum bid amount.

This situation would have been different had another bidder placed their bid before my bid. If another bidder had bid $5.00, the current bid would have changed to $5.00 which is the maximum proxy bid of the first bidder. When two members place a bid for the same amount, the bidder who placed their bid first becomes the high bidder.

The first bidder's bid was placed before the new $5.00 bid so the first bidder becomes high bidder at their $5.00 bid. Now I could not bid $5.01 because the current bid has changed and my $5.01 bid is below the minimum next bid amount. EBay would reject my bid if I attempted to place it now. I must bid the minimum increment above the current bid.

If this was confusing, don't worry about it. EBay handles all of this automatically you never have to calculate anything. Put in your snipe bid or your maximum proxy bid and fire it off. If there is a problem eBay will let you know.

What D' Ya' Bid?

How much do you pay for an auction?

It is important to do some research before placing a bid. Don't place a random bid and never bid $1 more than the current bid. Bidding the minimum or just above the minimum is a waste of time. You will never win an auction bidding this way. You will however drive up the price for no reason.

You need to know the retail price when buying a new item. There is no reason to buy a new item on eBay and pay retail price or higher. You are looking for a bargain. Don't buy it if you can't get a bargain.

Collectable prices are different. The real value is what you are willing to pay. You can look at past auctions for similar items to see what other people have paid, but the real value is *what is it worth to you*.

COMPARING PRICE

Is the opening bid a fair price, should I bid more or find another listing? I need to know what this item has been selling for in past auctions and what it is selling for in other current auctions. If it is a new item, what is the retail price? That will tell me the market value.

> *You can find past auction prices by searching for the keywords, then select the 'completed items' checkbox and click the Show Items button. This will show completed auctions and prices. Green prices are closed auctions that sold. Red prices are unsold items. You can also use Google.com to search for retail prices on new items.*

Check other current auctions and compare price and shipping. You can find other auctions by searching for keywords from the title of the auction you are looking at.

See if similar item auctions are a better deal or if the seller in another auction is more trustworthy. Never bid on an auction when you first see it. Jumping to bid before doing research can lead to disappointment and even fraud.

Make sure you read the entire description, shipping costs, and payment methods.

The chapter on Advanced Searching has more information on advanced searches. The **Don't Bid On It** video also has a demonstration showing how to research items.

If the item has several closed auctions with no sale, then there is no reason to pay a high Buy-It-Now price. You can bid the minimum and you will likely win because there has been no interest in past auctions. You may see the item has been relisted several times even after selling so the seller has a number of similar items.

If a seller keeps relisting the same item for $7 with no sales, you do not want to bid up to $20 for it when you can wait until the next auction.

Check other auctions by the same seller. The same item may have a Buy-It-Now price on another auction for the same price or even less.

DUTCH AUCTION

Dutch auctions are auctions where the seller is offering more than one of the same item. You can bid on one or more of the same items. You can buy one pillow or ten pillows. This seems to be confusing to many bidders. When you look at the bid history you will see many bidders bidding the maximum price. If a seller is selling multiples of an item, it means they have many to sell. Not all items will be sold at the highest price. If a seller has 20 handbags to sell and posts a Dutch auction for New Handbag $9.99, Quantity Available 20, it means there are 20 bags and they are available for $9.99 each. If one bidder bids $50 and nineteen other bidders bid $9.99, the first bidder receives one bag for $9.99 and all other bidders receive their bags for 9.99. This happens because the first bidder put in a $50 proxy bid, but the current high bid was only 9.99. Before bidding on a Dutch Auction, look at the bid history. There may be several bids, but there may be several items left and available for the opening bid amount. You can see several people bidding the minimum price which means you can win an item by simply bidding just higher than their bids. If you bid $10 and twenty other people bid $9.99, then you win a handbag for $9.99 along with nineteen other people and the last person to bid 9.99 is out.

This is not the same as selling multiple items in a Lot. Selling a Lot of items means selling several items in one auction to one buyer.

Dutch Auction – Cashmere Pillows $20 – 100 available
Lot Auction – Cashmere Pillows $200 for a case of 10 pillows

You never want to be the lowest or highest bidder in a Dutch Auction. Remember, this auction is for more than one item. The high bidder will win, but so will others as long as there are enough items to go around. You want to keep your bid just above the second lowest bid. This keeps you in the auction and paying the least amount.

This may seem confusing, but it is easy to remember that every bidder bids on a quantity and at the end of the auction, the available quantity is distributed among the high bidders, at the lowest bid price among them. Bid low on Dutch auctions, not high.

When using Snipe bidding software and there are many other bidders, place the snipe bid just below the high bid. This will keep your bid in the best range to win without bidding too much. If there are few bidders, bid in the middle of the bid range so you do not pay too much.

Reserve Auctions

Sellers can set a secret Reserve price when they setup an auction. This secret reserve is the price that must be met or exceeded by the bidding. If the secret Reserve is not met, the seller is not obligated to sell to the high bidder even if their bid is fair and they are willing to pay. Reserve auctions are discussed in more detail in the Seller section.

Bidders

Bidder_2
**I bid $150.55
I was high
bidder when
the auction
closed but I
still lost.**

Bidder_1
**I bid $100
which was
a fair price.
The auction
said my bid
did not meet
the reserve.**

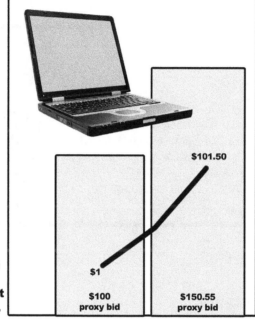

Seller

**Secret
Reserve
Price
$500**

$101.50

$1

$100
proxy bid

$150.55
proxy bid

$1 ——▶$101.50 ——▶ No Winner

Reserve Bidding Example

Our seller lists a laptop with an opening bid of $1 and sets a secret reserve price of $500. The seller is not afraid to start the bidding at $1 because he knows he will not have to sell unless the bids exceed $500. None of the bidders know what the secret reserve amount is. Bidder_1 bids $100 which he considered a fair price. This makes the current bid $1 which is the opening bid. One hundred dollars was less than the $500 reserve so Bidder_1 could never win the auction. Bidder_2 outbids Bidder_1 by placing a $150.55 bid. This is also below the secret reserve so Bidder_2 could never win the auction either. At the close of this auction there were no winners. Most reserve auctions close with no winner.

Odd-High Bids

Always bid odd-high amounts. Never bid 29.95 for an item. You do not want to bid an amount that is just below a round number amount like $30. Bid an odd-high amount like 31.55 or 31.05. Amateur bidders often bid in even amounts or they will add one cent in hopes of 'outbidding' others. If an item has a current bid of $10, an amateur bidder may bid $15 or $15.01 hoping to outbid anyone bidding $15 even. If you bid $15.07 or $15.63 you will be more likely to win this auction.

> *I found a game controller for 0.99 opening bid and 4.99 Buy-It-Now price with $8 shipping. There were 20 minutes before the end of the auction so I placed a bid of $2 trying to save a little money off of the BIN price. Twenty minutes later, there were four more bids and the final auction price was $7.25. Someone actually bid up a $4.99 controller to $7.25. The same seller had multiple listings and other sellers had similar listings offering the exact same item for $4.99 with a BIN price. This bidder overpaid for no reason. He did not bother to look at other auctions for the same item. I immediately went to another auction and purchased the same controller from the same seller for $4.99 plus $8 shipping and that was less than the high bidder paid on the first auction.*

Buyer Reality Check

There are thousands of rare items auctioned every year on eBay. The rare item you see now may show up weekly. You shouldn't feel that you have to buy this specific auction just because it is available. You may spend more than it is worth if you panic and over bid. Many rare items show up regularly on eBay.

An example is the Eldon Bowl-O-Matic. This is a toy bowling game. It commonly sells for $200 or more. It is very rare. It also shows up on eBay every three or four months. Just because you see something you want today does not mean that is the only time it will ever show up. There are many dealers, many people cleaning out attics, or thinning out collections to generate cash. Even rare collectables were produced in quantity at one time. It is very likely that another will show up. Before you become overly excited and bid a huge amount on that rare collectable, make sure you will be happy with the price. Check past auctions. You may be surprised to see others were sold or even went unsold recently.

Part II Buying
Chapter 8 - Evaluating Sellers

Once we find an item we are interested in, we must ask if we want to do business with this seller. There is no reason to look further into the auction if the seller cannot be trusted.

Do I want to buy from this seller? Are they trustworthy? I need to check their feedback history and look at several aspects of their auction to determine how trustworthy the seller is.

Shady Seller Check

Looking at the seller's feedback percentage is not enough. Many bidders mistakenly think the feedback percentage indicates the trustworthiness of the seller. The feedback percentage can be misleading. A highly rated seller with 100% positive feedback and 1000 transactions may look very trustworthy, but what if the account has been taken over by a criminal? You may not be buying from the person you thought you were.

Look at the seller's feedback. It is not unusual to have some negative comments, but sellers should not have too many. How many negatives have they received in the last month versus the number of sales they have made? The last 12 months? If the seller has a long history of positive feedback and suddenly they have 4 or 5 recent negatives, that may indicate the account has been hijacked by a criminal. A recent string of negative comments from different people is a bad sign.

What do the negative comments say? Are the people posting negative comments believable or just bad apples themselves? What is the feedback rating of those people leaving negative feedback? Just because a seller has a bad feedback rating or several over time does not mean the seller is dishonest or unreliable. Feedback comments from low rated members that say "*bad seller*" or "*where is my stuff*" can be ignored. Comments like these do not contain any details about the transaction. These terse comments usually indicate problem buyers. Comments like "*two weeks and no product, seller will not respond to email*" are much more informative. If a seller has a number of such comments, be careful about dealing with them.

Are those leaving the seller negative feedback themselves trustworthy? Feedback can tell a lot about a seller or buyer. Take a look at the feedback of those who left negative feedback. Do they have other negatives from sellers? Do they have a history of leaving negative feedback? Normally, eBay buyers should rarely need to leave negative feedback. Any buyer who makes a habit of leaving negative feedback should not be trusted.

When you are reading over the description, pay attention to what is listed and especially what is not listed. Is the seller offering a vintage radio without saying if it works or not? Is the seller explaining the rare mark on the bottom of a vase, but fails to show a photograph of it? Is the seller offering an expensive item with no photos or only blurry photos? It can be obvious if the seller is hiding something. Even if they are not intentionally hiding something, you can quickly figure out whether or not you want to do business with them. Dishonest or inexperienced, either way, sellers who hide important information are sellers to avoid.

Are there obvious misspellings or grammatical errors in the listing? Is the description IN ALL CAPITAL LETTERS? These are common signs of scam artists, children, or inexperienced sellers. Any auction with misspellings, all CAPS, or obvious grammatical errors should be avoided. People who speak English as a second language may have poor grammar, but you can recognize these auction listings because they are different from listings which simply have extremely poor grammar and poor communication skills.

Does the seller have a Reserve Price? Sellers with reserve prices are usually inexperienced. They frequently set unrealistic reserve prices so no one can win the auction. Avoid auctions with reserve prices.

Is there an unusual urgency in the auction? Scam artists often try to trick bidders into contacting them directly by using an urgent plea. They may claim they are moving out of the country, they are in a divorce, or they need surgery. They may have a Buy-It-Now price that sounds too good to be true or run a one day auction. All of these are warning signs that this seller should not be trusted.

Does the seller request, or even demand, that bidders contact them before bidding. This is a common scam. The dishonest sellers will offer the item at a bargain price to everyone who calls. They then take the money and disappear.

Does the seller make negative statements or threats in the listing? If the seller spoke to you in the tone of their auction, would you want to do business with them? Avoid sellers with bad attitudes or an axe to grind.

Does the seller list shipping costs? Beware of sellers who either do not state shipping costs or who list excessively high shipping. These are often signs of dishonest sellers who add inflated shipping after the auction closes or who try to offer a low price and charge excessive shipping to avoid eBay fees.

Does the seller say in the description or in the payment options they accept PayPal? If they have a large feedback rating and run auctions regularly, there is something not quite right about a regular seller who does not accept PayPal. Why can they not obtain a PayPal account? I don't trust big sellers who do not have PayPal accounts. Not having a PayPal account makes sending a payment more difficult and less reliable. Sellers who accept PayPal are always preferred over those who do not.

Where is the seller located? Is it local, is it in another country, do they hide where they are located? Never trust a seller who does not want anyone to know the general area or the country they are shipping from. The location is shown at the top of the auction. Beware of sellers who show USA as their location, but clearly do not speak English. These are frequently scammers in other countries who pretend to be in the USA.

Does the seller require or prefer an unusual payment method? Any seller who requests Western Union payments should not be trusted. Any seller asking for unusual payment methods or to use any payment website not on eBay's approved payment services list should be avoided.

Any seller who wants to use an escrow service other than escrow.com should be reported to eBay security. Escrow fraud is very common. Do not trust any member who wants to use a different escrow company.

If a seller requires payment by cash or cashier's check within three days and refuses common payment methods like PayPal or credit cards that is unusual. Cash type payment methods have no protection for the buyer. Beware of sellers offering expensive items who do not accept common forms of payment like PayPal or make unusual demands. Especially beware if they have few feedback ratings or bad feedback.

Is it too good to be true? Why is this seller $10 cheaper than anyone else? Is it worth $10 to risk being ripped off? It is better to pay a few dollars more and buy from a seller with a longer history and good feedback than it is to risk buying from a seller with no feedback history. I would say it is well worth it. Scammers make offers that are too good to be true.

Never buy from anyone with a zero feedback rating. When someone joins eBay, they naturally buy several items first and build some positive feedback before jumping in to sell. It looks fishy for someone to sign up and immediately post something for sale. I do not buy from anyone with less than ten feedback and they must have no negative feedback ratings if they only have ten. I do not buy expensive items from anyone with less than 20 or 30 feedback ratings. If they have any negatives it had better be early in their eBay career. Any other negatives and I will not buy from them. Generally I don't do business with anyone who has less than a 98% feedback rating.

In the seller's feedback section click on 'Feedback Left For Others' to see what feedback the seller has left. Do the comments sound intelligent or like they were made by a child? Does the seller leave any feedback for others? If they do not leave feedback then do you want to buy from a discourteous seller who does not respond to positive feedback from others? Does the seller leave retaliatory feedback for buyers who leave apparently legitimate negative feedback first? Does the seller have a lot of Mutual Withdrawals?

Use the Advanced Search feature to see the sellers past auctions. Has this seller been a buyer only, but now they suddenly have several auctions for expensive electronics? That is unusual. This seller's account may have been hijacked.

Has the seller previously been a buyer and seller of collector stamps, but now they have three auctions for three identical cars? It is very unusual for a stamp collector to suddenly jump into the car business. This also looks like a hijacked account.

Click on some of the sellers past auctions. Compare the description and terms. Are the old auctions clearly different from the current auction? Did the seller previously use good grammar and spelling, but their new auctions contain bad grammar or are in all CAPS? Has the seller been using plain auctions and now they are using lots of graphics? This is a clear sign that the account owner is not the person who posted the current auctions.

Has the seller's terms suddenly changed from past auctions? If the seller always accepted PayPal, but the new auctions do not accept PayPal, this may not be the account owner's auction.

Does the seller list a phone number in the auction with an area code different from the Location information at the top of the auction? You can Google search for 'area code 901' to find the city 901 is associated with. Scammers can setup VOIP telephone service anywhere, but they are not always so careful.

Does the seller list an email address in the auction and insist any contact is done through this email and not through eBay's Message Center? Scammers often do not change email contact information because the account holder will receive a notification that it has been changed. Scammers do not want bidders to use the Message Center because those messages can go to the real account owner. Scammers often demand bidders contact them through an email address directly.

When was the seller's account created? It is not normal for someone to setup an account and start selling immediately. Never buy from anyone who has not been a member of eBay for at least 3 months. Scammers often create accounts, build feedback in a short period and then begin running auctions to scam buyers. It is also very strange for any seller to build a lot of feedback in a short period. A series of feedback for 99 cent items is obvious, but these sellers can post fake auctions for high priced items and buy their own auctions using other fake accounts to build a good looking feedback history. They still do this in a short period of time so they are usually easy to spot.

Does the seller have other auctions for car stereos, tools, computers and jewelry? That sounds fishy to me and I would wonder if these items were stolen. That is an unusual

> *HiJacked!*
> *An eBay or PayPal account can be hijacked when a criminal obtains the user's password. The criminal will post fake auctions to scam other eBay members and may use a hijacked PayPal account to accept payments. Criminals often use look-alike eBay or PayPal websites to trick unsuspecting visitors into revealing their passwords. Family or friends can also hijack someone's account if they know the members password.*

group of items for someone to offer.

Has the seller been a buyer with a feedback rating of 10 and suddenly they have ten auctions for laptop computers with low Buy-It-Now prices or one day auctions? No one joins eBay and after ten buys suddenly starts selling ten laptop computers.

I'd rather give up the chance to win a low priced item than be ripped off by someone I should have known was a scammer. After checking all of these points we have to ask if we trust this seller. If we do not, then find another auction. If we do trust the seller, we can continue.

SHARED FEEDBACK

Look at a sellers feedback profile and compare the users who left feedback. Were all of the accounts that left feedback created at about the same time? Do they all have roughly the same feedback level? A seller with twenty feedback ratings from twenty different users that were created at the same time and who all have around 20 feedback is a sign of a scammer. The scammer created a number of accounts and used them to build fake feedback ratings for each other. The scammer will now use one as a seller account until it is disabled. Then they will use the next.

NEGATIVE FEEDBACK (UPDATE: eBay no longer allows sellers to leave negative feedback. This tip no longer applies but is left here in case they change that policy.)

I am extremely unlikely to bid against anyone with an overall negative feedback rating.
Billythenonpayingbidder1231(-2) - user has negative two rating
I know this is not the fault of the seller, but the seller should monitor their own auctions and cancel bids by any high bidder who has a negative rating. There is no reason to bid against someone who is not going to pay even if they win. This negative feedback person could have bid any amount and if I bid against them, I may be paying a lot more for an item than I should. Negative feedback buyers run up the price for the thrill of bidding. Bidding against them is foolish. When an auction is setup, the seller can block certain bidders. Sellers should setup their auctions to never allow negative feedback bidders.

GRAMMAR AND SPELLING

I NEVER BUY FROM ANYONE WHO POSTS AN AUCTION IN ALL CAPITAL LETTERS. The likelihood of problems with the transaction increases when you buy from someone who posts an auction in all capital letters. Posting an auction in all caps is not only a violation of Net Etiquette, but it is downright rude. All caps are considered SHOUTING on the Internet. No one wants to buy from someone who is shouting at them. When I first started using eBay, I would buy from sellers who used all caps. I quickly realized those auctions resulted in problems with the seller most of the time. Sometimes the seller did not described the item correctly, or they could not figure out how to cash a money order once they had it, or they packed the item poorly and it was broken. There is always a problem when dealing with an ALL CAPs seller.

Description
THIS ITEM IN VERY GOOD CONDTION. I AM MOVING AND MY SAYS I MUST SELL IT. THEIR IS NO PLACE FOR IT IN THE NEW HOUSE. I SHIP BY THE FAST MEANS IF YOU BUY BEFORE IT IS GONE.

Would you trust this seller? There are a number of warning signs here.

> *It is always inappropriate to post messages or auctions using all capital letters. That is SHOUTING and it is rude. ALL CAP auctions usually indicate an inexperienced person or a scammer trying to grab people's attention. Never buy from a seller who posts auctions in all caps.*

Intentional misspellings are sometimes appropriate. If a seller thinks there will be a common misspelling, they may use that in the title. People who search with the incorrect spelling will be able to find the item.

**Wizard Figurine Lead Casting, Fantasy Wizzard
Vintage Marilyn Monroe Calendar Claender Marylin**

This title has alternate common misspellings for Marilyn and Calendar. Placing alternate misspellings at the end of the title is common and accepted on eBay.

> *There is a caveat to the ALL CAPS rule. Terminals for the blind sometimes use all capital letters. If a blind person has such a terminal, they should set it to use all lower case instead. No one knows if an all caps auction came from a blind terminal and will assume it was by an inexperienced or unprofessional seller.*

Sellers who post in all CAPS, or cannot spell, or do not use correct grammar are more likely to be problem sellers or outright fraudulent sellers.

These sellers are usually young children, non-English speaking scammers, or simply incompetent sellers.

> *There is a caveat to the poor grammar rule. Deaf people, those that cannot hear and became deaf before they learned to speak, frequently have bad grammar. English is a spoken language and there are many nuances that are learned from speaking it. Deaf people never learned English by speaking it. There may be many deaf people with excellent grammar, but there are very intelligent deaf people with very poor grammar. With experience you can usually spot a post by a deaf person. It is different than a post by someone who learned English as a second language or a child. When you see a bad grammar post, keep in mind that it could have been posted by a deaf person.*

- Buying from incompetent sellers always leads to headaches. Many of the buyer complaints on the web involve buying from such people. Just like ALL CAP sellers, you may find the item is not as described, the person may not pack well, they may not ship on time or may not bother to check the auction status for weeks after it ends. By that time, they may have forgotten about it and not bother reading the email or payment notices. Poor spelling and grammar are clear signs of an incompetent seller or a scammer.
- You never want to buy from a young child. Young children do post items on eBay even though it is against eBay rules. Sometimes they have the items and sometimes they don't. They may ship the item or not. They have no repercussions if their account is disabled or they receive negative feedback so they may take advantage of this to scam a few people and make some money before their account is disabled. Poor spelling and grammar are common signs of an auction posted by a child.
- Scammers in other countries often pretend to be in the US and post fake auctions. These auctions may not always be high value items. Items costing $20 and $30 can represent big money in some countries, especially to small time criminals. These auctions can frequently be identified by poor grammar and good spelling. They will use a spell checker to make sure their auctions are spelled correctly, but they are not familiar with the English language so the bad grammar is a tip off. These people may mix up words like there-their, and your-you're because they pass a spell checker.

Read reports about auction fraud at www.auction-safety.org

Didn't Test It

If a seller says '*I didn't test it*' then you must ask yourself why not? Usually when a seller says they did not test something that can be easily tested, they are actually saying '*it does not work, but I don't want to admit it*'. Items like an MP3 player that can be easily tested, should be tested. Saying an item is untested can be a warning sign about the seller, but if you accept that the item is not working, and bid accordingly you can still come out with a good item you can repair or use for parts.

Ask The Seller

If you are still unsure about a seller, send them a question through the Ask Seller A Question link. Ask a legitimate question about the product or shipping. The seller's response may tell you a lot about him.

If the seller does not respond after a couple of days, then don't expect him to respond when you send payment either. You don't want to do business with someone like this. Never deal with a seller who ignores your legitimate questions.

Beware of any seller who responds with a form message or offers to sell the item at a fixed price outside eBay. Legitimate sellers will answer your question and will not offer to sell outside of eBay.

Ask Questions First

Make sure you ask any questions before you place a bid. If you are buying a collectable and its value is affected by the maker's stamp on the bottom, make sure there is a photo in the auction or ask the seller about it before placing a bid. If you are buying an Eldon Bowl-O-Matic bowling game toy, the auction should say whether or not it includes the bowling pins, does it include the bowling ball, or the box, does it work? All of these factors affect the value. Missing parts may be impossible to replace. An original box in good shape can sometimes be worth more than a collectable toy. If the seller does not answer your questions in the auction listing, ask them through eBay's Message Center.

Pre-Bidder Approval

Auction statements like "All Buyers must contact me before bidding" are sure signs the seller is attempting to make a sale outside of eBay. Sellers like this cannot be trusted because they may sell the same item to several people with none of them receiving anything. Why would a seller need buyers to contact him before bidding? If there are special bidding terms then why are they not listed? You cannot trust sellers who require pre-contact. EBay knows about these types of phrases and will remove such auctions when they are reported.

> *Pre-approved Bidders are used on legitimate auctions for high value items. If the seller adds the bidder to the approved bidder list then the auction sounds legitimate. If the seller makes an offer to sell the item outside of eBay, then the auction is a scam. Legitimate sellers will never use Bidder Pre-approval to sell an item outside of eBay.*

EBay has strict rules against selling an auctioned item outside of eBay. Some sellers will offer an item for auction and in the listing say they will sell at a certain price to the first person who contacts them. Selling an item that has been listed without allowing the auction to complete is unfair to bidders and a violation of eBay rules

Some sellers of big ticket items list them, then sell them outside of eBay and cancel the listing to avoid eBay fees. This is not uncommon in antiques and collectables that are expensive. A seller can list an auction then put their email address in the auction, perhaps imply they have other items to sell too. They may leave out a critical part of the description and then invite people to call or email for that information. They may even blatantly state bidders must contact them before bidding without saying in so many words they will sell direct. This is a sure sign the seller wants to make a backdoor deal. Then when a buyer contacts them, the seller makes an offer. They sell directly and cancel the auction. EBay is wise to this and will cancel the accounts of buyers or sellers they suspect are selling outside of eBay. Selling outside of eBay is not in the buyer's or the seller's interest. Some sellers may think they are saving a few dollars in eBay fees, but the eBay fees are so small they are not important. It is completely unfair to the people who were interested in bidding and it is a poor business move because they item may have been bid higher than what the seller negotiated in the direct sale. Outside-of-eBay sales are a common tactic used by scammers. They will post an auction and offer a direct sale. They then sell to several people, but never ship anything. Never trust a seller who is willing to sell outside of eBay.

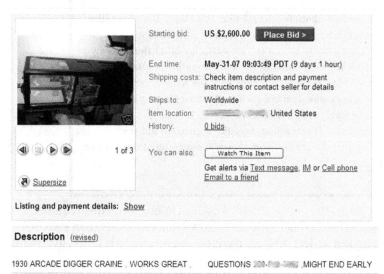

Example of a seller trying to make a deal outside of eBay. This seller is offering an expensive item but, they give no details which forces interested buyers to contact them. They provide a phone number to avoid the eBay Message Center. They also used poor photographs so interested buyers must ask questions. Another warning sign is the ALL CAPS description. Is this seller selling one to one person or will they offer the same item at a 'discount' to several people without ever shipping anything?

Due Diligence – The Seven Keys to Avoid Being Scammed

You must practice due diligence before bidding on an auction. This means using some common sense before giving away your hard earned money.

1. **Research** – Make sure you read the description of the item and understand if there are any flaws. Can you live with the flaws or condition? Make sure you research the item and its value. You need to check past auctions to see what this item has sold for. Is it a lot more or a lot less than the current item? Why? Make sure you understand what you are buying. Some items like coins, stamps, and comic books have detailed grading standards and the condition can be the difference between a collectable and drawer filler. Know your category and your item before you bid.

2. **Seller Check** – Check out the seller. Read the description. Does it sound like it was written by a child? Is the spelling and grammar correct? Does the seller threaten potential buyers or make unreasonable or unusual demands? Is this someone you would want to do business with? Check their feedback. What do buyers say, both good and bad. Do they have a lot of recent negatives? What other items are they selling? Have they been a buyer with a feedback of +10 and now they are suddenly selling twenty laptop computers?

3. Does the seller offer to sell direct outside of eBay? Honest sellers do not sell outside of eBay.

4. **Photo** – Is there a photo for the auction, is it clear? Does the seller mention a scratch or damage, but not show a photo of it?

5. Does the seller want to use an escrow company other than escrow. com? Escrow scams are among the most common on eBay.

6. **Payments** – What payment methods does the seller accept? Beware of sellers who demand cash or Western Union payments. Do they take PayPal? If not then why not?

7. **Communication** – If you asked the seller a question did they respond? If they do not respond, they will not respond if you have a problem.

Beware of any auction that states they only accept Western Union payments, requires cash payments, or where the seller wants to use an escrow company other than escrow. com. Those are always dishonest sellers. Once a payment is sent, there is no recovering it when the seller disappears.

Remember, if it sounds too good to be true, it is.

PART II BUYING
CHAPTER 9 - BIDDING STRATEGIES

DON'T BID EARLY OR HIGH

Only amateur bidders bid early. Amateur bidders frequently bid early and either bid just above the minimum or bid a high amount. Never bid early or high. Bidding early invites thrill bidders to compete against you. They will bid items up by $1 and $2 again and again until they become high bidders which runs the price way up. They may have no intention of paying for the auction if they should win, but they have cost the final bidder more money. This is why you should not bid high and early. Bidding high simply makes the game more fun for the thrill bidder.

AVOID BIDDING WARS

Bidding wars start when bidders become emotionally involved in the bid process. One person is outbid and returns to bid a few dollars more. When the proxy bid of the other bidder immediately outbids them, they bid again and again until they become high bidder. They lose sight of the value of the item and are concerned only with winning. This type of emotional bidding is what sellers want. It pushes auction prices above the value of the item and makes lots of money for sellers. It also means the final high bidder has paid a lot more for the auction than they had to. If this bidder had simply placed a snipe bid in the final seconds of the auction and let the other bidder enjoy being high bidder until the end, they could have jumped in, placed their bid, outbid the amateur bidder who placed a bid lower than they were willing to pay, and become the winner of the auction.

You can check the bid history on an item to see if other bidders are already involved in a bidding war. If you see the same two or three bidders re-bidding over and over, this item is one to avoid. If you are interested, put in a snipe bid for a fair amount near the auction end time and don't worry about watching the auction. If the other bidders do not run the price up too much, maybe you can win. Most likely they will run up the price to double or triple the actual value in a blind attempt to win.

This may be an opportunity. When the auction closes at an outrageously high price, contact the seller and say you missed the end of the auction. Then offer to buy at your bid price if the high bidder does not come through. If the high bidder was emotionally driven, they may back out or simply not pay. In this case the seller may be glad to sell to someone who will pay even if it is less than the high bid. The seller may not think about a second chance offer to the second high bidder, but will remember your offer to buy.

Holiday Bargains

Look for bargains during holidays and holiday weekends. During holidays many people are busy with other events or away from home. This is a good time to pick up bargains with less competition.

Snipe Bidding

Snipe Bidding is the secret to winning auctions. A Snipe Bid is a bid placed in the final seconds of an auction. When an eBay auction's end time arrives, it is over. There is no extension and no waiting for last minute bids. By placing a bid in the final seconds, other bidders are prevented from re-bidding. This gives experienced bidders an advantage over amateur bidders. Amateur bidders will bid early and low amounts. When they are outbid, they will return and bid a few dollars more over and over. The experienced bidder uses snipe bidding software to automatically place their bid for maximum amount they are willing to pay in the final seconds of the auction.

Snipe Bidding allows the experienced bidder to avoid bidding wars.

Many amateur bidders also do not understand pricing or valuation. They will see an item at a low price and bid. They have no idea what the real value of the item is and they do no research to see what the item has previously sold for. They think the price is a bargain so they bid. When they are outbid they may return and bid several more times to remain high bidder. Without knowing the value of the item, they can bid more than it is worth. They will frequently bid more than they ever would have considered bidding if the item had an opening bid of the same price they just bid.

This bidding frenzy is great for sellers because they can sell items for more than their value. It is not a good situation for bidders. The amateur bidder who keeps running up the price may eventually win, but they now have to pay a lot more than they wanted for their 'bargain'.

Let amateur bidders place their early and low bids and remain high bidders. When the end of the auction approaches, the snipe software will place the bids of the experienced bidders and the amateur bidder will be immediately outbid without running up the price in unnecessary bidding wars.

Some people may think this is unfair, but in the auction winner was the person who put in the highest bid. The amateur bidder cannot depend on the opportunity to change their mind about their bid. Frequently, the amateur bidder will put in a low bid, maybe far below market value, for the item so they could not realistically expect to win anyway. The experienced bidder will put in a serious bid for the maximum they were willing to pay. Ultimately, the high bidder won.

Snipe bid amounts are chosen with a cool head and after doing price research on the item.

The snipe bidder knows what price they are willing to pay and sets that price in their software. In the final seconds of the auction, the software will automatically place the bid for the bidder. There is no risk of emotional or irrational bidding when using Snipe Bidding.

Snipe Bidding is not a guarantee to win. The high bidder is the winner, not the last bidder. Snipe bidding has been shown mathematically by statistical analysis to be highly effective. Even without the mathematical analysis, experienced eBay bidders have long known it is effective. That is why they use it.

You can find detailed information on how snipe bidding works and the mathematics behind it at http://www.snipe-to-win.com. You can also find Snipe Bidding software there.

See Appendix B for more information on how Snipe Bidding works.

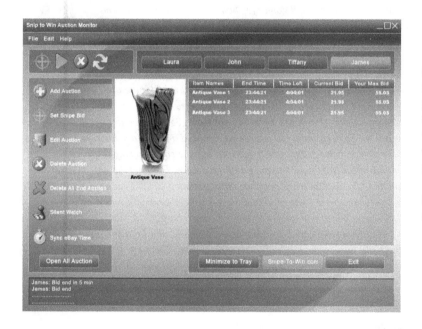

Snipe Bidding Software places your bid in the final seconds of the auction which avoids bidding wars which run up the price.

Snipe-To-Win.com software pictured.

SURLY BIDDERS

A surly bidder will bid against another bidder out of personal motivation and not for the item. They can be motivated by spite, jealousy or bitterness. If you outbid another bidder in an auction and they see your auction ID in another auction, they bid simply to run up the price against you. Surly bidders are motivated to harm other members by running up the price or depriving them of an item. This is another reason to use snipe bidding or at least bid as close to the end of the auction as possible.

There are three types of bids whether placed by proxy or snipe.

- **Cool-to-Win** – Cool to have that item at a super bargain price
- **Like-to-Win** – I need this, but only at the right price
- **Have-to-Win** – I have to win this even if I pay more than the market value

COOL-TO-WIN

A Cool-To-Win bid is a low bid on something that you would not mind having at your bid price, but you would not pay more for it. I lose these auctions most of the time. I lose them because I am looking for a super bargain and my bids are very low. When I do win, it is great because I have a true bargain. I have bid pennies on the dollar and won.

When the movie Pirates of the Caribbean came out, a company started producing Pirates of the Caribbean themed pinball games for home use. These were around $500 and they were terrible. They were overpriced and cheaply made. It was easy to find bad reviews on the Internet for the game. The company had warehouses of these games they could not unload. The price started dropping and eventually they sold out to liquidators. These liquidators began offering the games for $0.99 on eBay with $65 shipping. They were making the minimum they needed on shipping and any bids that raised the price were gravy. I knew the games were not popular, but I wanted one just to play around with. It was certainly not worth $500 to me, not worth $100 to me either. But for $65 shipping, I'm interested. I placed a bid on one auction and was out bid. The company was running ten auctions at once so I setup my snipe software to bid on all of them at $5 plus shipping until I won one. Finally I did win one for $1.60 in a late night auction when only one other person bid. I did not need this pinball game, but for the price I was glad to have it. I saw other auctions closing for $50 to $150. If I win a cool-to-win auction, I know I have a bargain. If I lost all of the auctions then I would not have cared. I would have saved $70. But I did win and I won something that I will gain more than $70 in enjoyment from. This item was Cool-To-Win at the price. It was not something I really needed, but it was something fun.

Pirates of the Caribbean: Dead Mans Chest Pinball

Seller of this item? Sign in for your status

Starting bid:	US $0.99 Place Bid >
End time:	May-18-07 10:57:17 PDT (1 day 3 hours)
Shipping costs:	US $65.00 Standard Flat Rate Shipping Service Service to United States
Ships to:	United States
Item location:	MCKINNEY TX, United States
History:	0 bids
You can also:	Watch This Item

View larger picture

Get alerts via Text message, IM or Cell phone
Email to a friend

I look for super bargains when I place my Cool-To-Win bids. I picked up this home pinball game for $1.60 plus $65 shipping.

HAVE-TO-WIN

Have-To-Win. These are items that you really want and cannot live without. Usually these are collectables that do not show up often. The idea behind Have-To-Win bids is to power bid your way to a win. You bid more than you think the item is worth, much more than the market price, to guarantee you will win. You should not look at every auction as a Have-To-Win. This is reserved for those special auctions and rare items that are truly important to you.

> *While I was researching for a book, I found an antique catalog of arcade games on eBay. I wanted this catalog. I really wanted it. I knew I had to win this item. The opening bid was $9.99 I could have put in a bid of $20, or $50 or $100. But, I had to win this item. I was not willing to lose it. I bid $255.55 for a 30 page catalog. I thought this was outrageous and no one would come close to it. I would not be thrilled to pay that much, but if I had to then I would. After all, I was planning to use it in a book and it would add value to my book which would mean I could recoup the money on book sales. In the final seconds of the auction my snipe software placed the bid. The auction closed at $255.55. The second high snipe bidder put in $255.50. I won the auction by five cents. It turned out other collectors really wanted this item too, but I won. I put in a ridiculous amount and in the end I had to pay it. This was fine with me, I had the item I really wanted and even though I would have preferred to pay less I was still happy to win. Most of the time when I do this, I do not lose and I do not have to pay my maximum either. I pay more than the value of the item, but I pay what it is worth to me. I was able to make money from my purchase so ultimately it was an investment and not shelf decoration. If I were looking for shelf decoration, I would not have put in such a strong bid.*

Remember, never bid more than you can afford. Bid an amount you will be happy to pay if you should win.

LIKE-TO-WIN

A Like-To-Win auction is one where the item is something you would like to have, but only at the right price. It may be a new item that is frequently available for auction or an item you would like to add to a collection if it is cheap. If you are thinking *"I would like to win this item, but only if the price is right"* then you have a Like-To-Win scenario. It is best to avoid becoming emotionally attached to an item. You may bid too much for it and find a week or month later the same item has sold a number of times for much less than you paid. Bid an amount that you would be happy to pay, including shipping, for the item and no more. If you are looking for a bargain, set your price accordingly. If you do not win the item, simply look for another listing and try again until you win at a price you are willing to pay. The game of finding an item at the price you want can be more enjoyable than the item itself.

Once you have decided how badly you want the item and if you are looking for a bargain price or a market price, you will be ready to do some more analysis. I told you auctions were fun.

Risk Strategy

Buying collectables involves some degree of risk. This is especially true for items that have wide value ranges or knock-offs. Suppose you want to bid on a Tiffany type lamp. The seller is not familiar with lamps and cannot confirm whether or not it is an original Tiffany or a knock-off. You are afraid to ask the buyer too many questions because they have previously posted responses to questions in the auction and may reveal the answer. If it is real it may be worth $1000. If it is a knock-off it may be worth $120. How much do you bid?

You do not want your valuation to be too high. If others also think it is real, the price will close very high. You do not want to spend $1000 on it because you could buy a known real Tiffany lamp for the same price. You also do not want to miss a real lamp at a bargain price. Your price choice will depend on your knowledge of the market. If it is the real thing and no one else bids, you may have a bargain. If it is not an original and other bidders bid up the price thinking it is real, you may be overpaying a lot. If you are looking for a bargain and are willing to take a risk, you will have to pick a price between the best and worst case values.

You must ask yourself if you can accept the loss should you be wrong and the item is not valuable. You may be paying $500 for a $120 lamp or $500 for a $1000 lamp. Is receiving a $120 lamp worth the risk? Only you can answer this question.

Nervous Sellers

A seller can revise the auction and raise the minimum bid up to 12 hours before the auction closes if there are no bidders. A nervous seller may become worried that there will be no bids and want to increase the opening bid to protect his investment. By placing a bid for the minimum amount, you prevent the nervous seller from changing the opening bid to a higher value. If you think the seller may revise their minimum bid, place a minimum bid early. Then later you can place your real bid as close to the end of the auction as possible or using your snipe bidding software.

Best Offer Strategy

When you see someone selling an item for a buy now price with a *best offer* option and it looks like the person sells many of the same item, always check completed auctions for the last sale price. Sellers can set a value where offers are automatically accepted if they are above a certain price. This means instead of paying $44 for an item, you can make an offer for $37 and have it immediately accepted if the buyer has set the item to accept offers of that value. I was interested in a lens filter for my camera. The one I wanted was $44.95 but the seller had a best-offer offer. I checked past auctions by selecting the Completed Auctions option and saw that the same item was sold by the same seller for $37. I then knew he would sell at that level. I made an offer and it was immediately accepted. I just saved $8 by a few seconds of research. I could have also tried an offer at $20 first, but from past auctions it was clear $37 was his minimum that was accepted.

Auctions that list a Buy-It-Now price can be purchased immediately at the listed price. There is no bidding for Buy-It-Now items. They have a single fixed price which may or may not be combined with an opening bid..

Buyers may not want to wait until the end of an auction. They may consider it worth the extra money to avoid waiting until the end of the auction. Sometimes you want to find a good price and Buy-It-Now. If I see a book advertised and I find it on eBay, I want it right then. There is no point in waiting seven days for the end of a $10 auction. If I find the item I want, I compare prices, shipping, seller ratings and use the buy now option. Buy-It-Now is perfect for new items with established values.

Sellers can combine Buy-It-Now and auctions. The BIN price is only available until a bid is placed.

Buy-It-Now gives the smart bidder an advantage in auctions. If you find an item with a high Buy-It-Now price and low opening bid, you can bid the minimum amount to knock out the Buy-It-Now price. This will give you the chance to bid on it later using your maximum bid through snipe bidding software.

You no longer risk someone else using the Buy-It-Now option ending the auction.

> *I once saw a rare arcade game (it was MCI's The Safe produced in 1974) offered with an opening bid of $200 and a Buy-It-Now price of $600. I did not want to pay $600, so I placed a $200 bid to knock out the Buy-It-Now price. I set my snipe software to bid $405.55 and won the auction for $360. I saved $240 which almost covered the shipping costs. Knocking out the BIN price is not a guarantee that the item will close lower. Sometimes it does close higher than the BIN price. I was lucky to save so much on this auction by knocking out the Buy-It Now price*

MARKET FLOOR BIDDING

This is a bidding technique I sometimes use. It is not a way to win an item, but a way to generate value within a market. Suppose you own a very rare Civil War medal. You know there are less than twenty in existence. One appears for auction. Bidding is slow because very few people know what the item is or how valuable it is. You do not need the medal because you already have one, but you bid anyway. This bid is not meant to win the item, but to set a bottom price, a market floor. If your bid is the high bid then you will have to buy the item. The bidder generally hopes to be outbid. If anyone else wants the item they will have to top your high bid. This technique is can be compared to setting a reserve on someone else's auction. The only difference is that you wind up buying the item if no other buyer is willing to pay the market-floor price for it. By setting a market floor bid, you maintain a bottom limit value on the item. This makes the overall market more valuable, or at least it appears more valuable. If another medal comes up for auction, then it may sell for more which then makes the items more valuable in the real market. Is this ethical? As long as the person placing the bid is willing to pay for the item, then it is ethical. I have used this technique in the antique arcade groups to maintain the value of several very rare items.

If I see a particularly rare item appear that I already own, I will place a bid even if I do not want the item. This keeps the market high. This is one time when bidding early and letting other collectors see your bid is desirable. Other collectors see my interest and begin bidding against me. Eventually they win the item. If there are only one or two other bidders, I know I have increased the market value of the item. If I should win the item then I pay for it and add it to my collection or try to resell it on eBay. This is not surly bidding. Surly bidding is placing a bid on an item to keep anyone else from obtaining it at a bargain price. The difference is the bidder's motivation as to whether it is surly or market-floor bidding.

Market Floor bidding may lead to a collector attempting to corner the market. If the bidder accidentally buys one or two pieces, they may begin intentionally buying. If there are a limited number of rare collectables available, the collector may buy every available piece simply to reduce supply and therefore make their collection more valuable.

MARKING THE AUCTION

What if you think the seller is legitimate, but you suspect the seller may sell it outside of eBay(seller may state they are offering the item locally and plan to cancel the auction early)? Ebay does allow auctions to be cancelled for local sales as long as the sale did not result from someone seeing the eBay listing. When you see an auction for an item you want and there are no bids and no Buy-It-Now price, you should enter the minimum bid. This is called Marking-The-Auction. This is a time when you want to make a minimum bid.

If someone else bids against you and becomes high bidder, that is great. Let them be high bidder for a while. When your snipe bid is placed then you will see who wins.

By putting in your bid, you make it known that you are interested in this item so the seller will be less likely to cancel the item and you can complain to eBay if they do cancel the auction. It is hard to complain if there are no bids and the seller cancels the auction you were watching. It is unfair to interested bidders to cancel an auction early.

BIDDER RESEARCH

You may have heard about techniques for researching the habits of other bidders to gain an advantage. This is a waste of time. The serious bidders will use snipe software to place their bids in the final seconds of the auction. You will not even know who they are until the auction is over. It does not matter who the current high bidder is.

Researching the current high bidder may tell you that they return at 5 PM every day to re-bid if they are out bid, but does this really help? Why would you want to bid against them and drive up the price of the auction? Why would you want to slip in your bid just after their normal bidding time, raising the price, when the real bids will be placed in the final seconds of the auction anyway? When you use snipe bidding, none of the bidder research matters. The only bids that matter are the ones in the final seconds and you don't know who will place those until the end of the auction.

There is one type of bidder research which can be helpful. Suppose you are interested in an item and you see **ebaybidder1234(7)** is the current high bidder with three days to go in the auction and a high bid of $10. You can use the advanced search feature to see what auctions this bidder has bid on recently. You can see not only auctions they won but auctions they lost. This will show you if this person has bid on similar items and what their maximum bid was. You can expect their proxy bid on this item to be close if they have bid on similar items in the past. If **ebaybidder1234(7)** has bid on three past auctions for the same item and their bids were $40, $37, and $37.55 you can expect the current auction proxy bid is actually around $40.

You can also identify snipe bidders on past similar auctions.

If a similar auction closed a week ago with two snipe bidders bidding $100 and $200 with the $200 bidder winning, you know there is someone out there willing to bid $100 and they are likely to snipe the auction at the last minute. The $200 bidder already won his auction and is unlikely to rebid on the same collectable. This would indicate you should bid over $100 with your snipe bid. If you bid less and this second $100 bidder wins, you may be able to pickup the next auction at a lower price as long as no new collectors become interested.

This research will give you an idea of what to expect in the current auction. EBay may hide the bidder's identities on high value items which can make researching specific bidders more difficult.

No-Bid Bargains

You can sometimes find bargains on items that have received no bids. Some sellers may offer an item at a low opening bid, but there is no interest or there may be a misspelling in the title that prevents interested buyers from finding the auction. Pick a category that is of interest to you and select the sort option to show 'Time Ending Soonest'. This will sort the listings and show you the items that are about to close. You can look for items that have no bids and very low opening bid prices. Always use due diligence and check the auction terms as well as the seller feedback before bidding. There may be a good reason that there are no bids on an item, such as a dishonest seller, excessive shipping charges, or strange seller terms.

Take Advantage of Bad Auctions

Many sellers inadvertently do things that drive away potential bidders. Some of these sellers are dishonest and should be ignored. Some are simply inexperienced which can present an opportunity for a bargain.

It can really be a great opportunity with little risk if you can pick up the item locally. This allows you to see what you are buying before paying.

Look for auctions with big seller mistakes. Poor photos or no photo auctions keep prices down and you may find these have no other bidders at the end of the auction. You do run the risk of dealing with a problem seller or misrepresented item, but if you are a bargain hunter, it can be worth the occasional headaches. When you find an auction like this, never bid a fair market price, always bid low, really low. Try to snap it up at a super cheap price.

If the opening bid is too high, you can wait to see if there are any bidders. You can contact these sellers after the auction ends if there are no bidders and make an offer. This is not the same as selling outside of eBay because the auction did run its course. EBay may still object so word your offer carefully.

When do you bid the minimum amount?
Generally you will not bid the minimum or opening bid amount, but there are always exceptions to any good rule.

Bid the minimum when
- *An auction is about to end with no bidders and you want to win the item at a bargain price*
- *You suspect a legitimate seller may sell the item locally and cancel the auction if there are no bids on it*
- *You suspect a seller may revise the auction listing if there are no bids on the final day of the listing and raise the opening bid amount.*

CHAPTER 10 - WIN, LOSE, OR DRAW?

END OF AUCTION TIME

You won the auction! What now?

First, congratulate yourself on a good job. You did your research on the item and the seller. You have confidence in the value of the item and in the trustworthiness of the seller. You bid a price that you knew you would be happy with and now you will soon have something you need or wanted really badly.

You will receive an email notice from eBay and possibly the seller when you win an auction. You can return to eBay, find the auction in your MyEBay page under Won Auctions, where you can click the Pay Now button to pay. If the seller set up their auction correctly, this should be all there is to it. Using this button also assures that you will be transferred to the real PayPal website to complete the payment.

If you did not win the item, you will receive an email from eBay saying you were outbid or the reserve price was not met.

You can always see if you won or lost an auction by checking your MyEBay page. It lists won auctions, lost auctions, and auctions you are currently bidding on.

Make sure you send the correct payment amount and include shipping charges. You can include insurance if it is offered. Double check your shipping address and give a phone number in the payment comment box so the seller can contact you if there are any problems.

Include a printout of the auction or a copy of the end of auction email if you send payment by money order. The seller may have many auctions running. He will have no way of knowing what this money order marked 'eBay purchase' is for. If the seller has twenty items at $20 Buy-It-Now prices, then he will receive a lot of $20 payments. A seller has no way of knowing who paid for what if he receives a $20 money order in the mail with no information. Even if there is a shipping address, he does not know what item to ship or which eBay ID sent the payment. Include a print out if you are mailing in a payment so the seller knows who is paying for what.

> *I have received many money orders in envelopes with illegible return addresses and no other information. I had no way of knowing what the payment was for or who sent it. These payments go on top of a filing cabinet and sit there until someone emails asking if I received their money order.*

Now sit back and wait a reasonable time until your order arrives. In the US, orders should arrive in a week or so. Orders shipped from outside the USA may take up to a couple of weeks.

If you forget to pay and receive a payment reminder, contact the seller immediately and send payment by PayPal. Let the seller know that you forgot or did not realize you won the auction. Mailing a payment without telling the seller it is on the way is a mistake. When the seller does not hear from the buyer, he will assume the buyer is not planning to pay and may re-auction the item.

One of the worst things to do is wait a month and then complain to the seller that the item did not arrive. That is much too long to wait. Contact the seller and let them know you have not received the item and need the tracking information or ship date and expected delivery date if the item did not arrive within a reasonable time. If you paid for Priority Mail shipping then you can expect the item to arrive within a week. Don't let your emotions build up as you check the mail every day only to find disappointment. There is no reason to wait a month before complaining angrily to the seller about a package that should have shipped by Priority Mail. You may find that the item was lost in the mail, or that the seller did not know your PayPal payment was sent, or any other legitimate reason. You may even find that the item was delivered weeks ago and your spouse put it on a shelf somewhere. This happened to me a number of times. A bidder waits weeks after they should have received an item before angrily complaining. I check the tracking and see the item was delivered weeks ago. Then the bidder sends an apology saying the item was in their office the whole time or it was on their porch, or their child had it.

> *I have found that 99% of the time, when I email to ask the status or complain about an expected item not arriving, it arrives within one or two days. I try to be patient for a couple of extra days now.*

If you do need to contact the seller, use the eBay Message center under your MyEBay page. Make sure you include the item number and description. If you contact the seller directly by email, include the item number and description.

Once you receive the item you can check it over and if it is as described in the auction, leave positive feedback for the seller.

If you did not receive the item and you were unable to contact the seller, or they refused to ship an item you paid for, you can file a Seller Non-Performance notice. There is a shortcut to this page at http://portal.dont-bid-on-it.com

WHAT IF YOU LOST?

It happens. You cannot win every auction. Look for a similar item or add the keywords to your favorite search list to be notified when a similar item is relisted. You can try bidding again. Repeat your price research and see if you are bidding close to the market value for the item. You cannot expect to win a $500 item for $50. If you see similar auctions close at $50 and your last auction was bid up to $75, it could be a fluke or the item may have been in better condition. Keep trying and watch for the next auction.

When you are outbid at the end of an auction and the winner edges out your maximum bid by $1, don't think you lost by $1. The high bidder may have actually bid $100 more than your high bid. EBay's proxy bidding system only increases the high bid by the minimum bid amount. Even if you had bid $2 more, you may not have become high bidder.

Make sure the maximum bid you put in is one you are comfortable with. If you lose then you would not have been happy to win at a higher price either so the auction is best lost. Watch for the next auction and try again.

RESPONSIBILITY

If the buyer purchases an item and finds out the seller failed to disclose pre-existing damage, or the item that was listed as working does not work, then they have a reason to return the item for a refund. This is the seller's fault. If the item was damaged in shipping it is not the sellers fault unless it was poorly packaged. If the buyer receives their item and realizes they did not read the description thoroughly, or they change their mind, that is not the seller's responsibility and the seller is not required to accept a return. If the buyer finds a better price elsewhere or in another auction, the seller is not obligated to accept a return and an honest buyer would not even ask.

PART III COMMUNITY RESPONSIBILITIES
CHAPTER 11 - FEEDBACK

Feedback is the method used to rate a buyer or seller. Good buyers and sellers receive positive feedback from members they buy from or sell to. Bad members receive negative feedback. Wait a minute...that is not right. That is how it used to work but not now.

EBay uses a feedback system to show how many successful transactions a user has completed. Both the buyer and seller can leave feedback for each other. Sellers can only leave positive feedback. EBay had a problem with sellers leaving retaliatory negative feedback for buyers who left negative feedback. This was a complicated situation. Many buyers left unfair negative feedback for sellers which deserved return negative feedback. But, sellers who did scam buyers could threaten negative feedback to prevent the buyer from leaving honest negative feedback. This made the feedback system unreliable.

Now the system allows buyers to leave sellers negative feedback, but sellers can only leave positive feedback for buyers. This would appear to protect dishonest buyers, but eBay considers the three strike rule as compensation for this. When a seller reports a auction as unpaid and it is not paid through PayPal, the buyer receives an unpaid item strike. Three of these and the buyer has his or her account blocked. In eBay's opinion, sellers have no need to leave negative feedback because problem buyers will be blocked. Unfortunately this also assumes non-paying buyers are the only type of dishonest buyer. This is not the case. There are many kinds of dishonest buyers including those who threaten negative feedback unless they receive some additional item or a partial refund without justification, buyers who buy a new item and return a broken used item demanding a refund, etc.

The feedback system also has some improvements. It only counts feedback received in the past 12 months. Previously one negative feedback would follow you for life. This is no longer the case. If you are an active seller then you will have multiple accounts anyway. If you receive undeserved feedback, simply switch to another standby seller account. In 12 months start using the account to make purchases and you will begin to receive feedback from sellers which gives you a positive rating(pick a seller who always leaves positive feedback or a big seller who uses an automated feedback response system) you can switch back and now have 100% positive feedback. An occasional negative from a flake customer is not a problem anymore either. Buyers(at least intelligent ones which are the ones you want to deal with) understand that there are a few flaky people on eBay who leave negative feedback for no reason. One or two negatives among a large number of positives do not hurt your sales.

◯ Game came finally! Thank you!		Buyer: alisemsmith (133 ☆)	May-17-07 08:48
ROBOTECH INVASION XBOX SHOOTER GAME NEW AND SEALED (#230127133887)		US $0.01	View Item

Example of Feedback posted after buyer received the item

You cannot leave feedback for just anyone; it is only between the buyer and seller. A buyer who buys from a seller and never receives anything can leave negative feedback for that seller to warn other potential buyers that the seller takes the money and never ships anything. When a user has too many negative feedback ratings, eBay can disable their account.

You do not have to worry about retaliatory negative feedback from sellers anymore but this does not mean you should leave negative feedback immediately. Most problems can be easily worked out by contacting the seller first. I consider any buyer who leaves me negative feedback without contacting me first in an honest effrrt to resovle a problem to be dishonest. There are people on eBay who simply get a thrill out of leaving negative feedback and look for opportunities. I had one woman leave me negative feedback because she bid more than the retail price for an item. I had nothing to do with her choice to pay more than she could have bought the item for on the Internet, she never asked to cancel the auction, yet she still left me negative feedback blaming me for her own failure to do any price research before bidding.

When a buyer does not pay for an item and the seller files an unpaid item notification with eBay, the buyer can still leave feedback, but that feedback is not counted in the seller's history and is removed when the buyer does not pay after a certain number of days. If the seller had not filed the unpaid claim then the buyer could have threatened negative feedback to extort the item from the seller or simply have left mean spirited negative feedback for the seller even though the buyer was the one at fault.

Sellers can not file false unpaid notices because PayPal payment status is available to eBay. If a seller files a false notice and the buyer proves they did pay, it could be the seller who has their account suspended for filing false unpaid item notices.

If you do have a problem with a seller, make sure you contact the seller through the eBay message console before leaving feedback. The item may have been lost in shipping or the seller may have made an honest mistake and forgot to ship it. Even if you believe the item is not as described, you should give the seller an opportunity to make it right or accept the returned item for a refund. You do not want to leave negative feedback without giving the seller an opportunity to resolve the matter first. That is simply dishonest.

I once purchased a camera lens on eBay. I did not realize it would not fit my camera until after I received it. I relisted it on eBay to sell it. The buyer received it and emailed back that it was unusable because it was a sealed lens and there was mold growing in it. I never attached the lens to my camera so I did not know about the mold. I issued the buyer a refund and told him to keep the lens. It was not worth the trouble to have him return a $30 lens and pay shipping on it. This was a simple matter that was easily resolved when the buyer contacted the seller first.

Who Gets What Feedback?

Positive Feedback – For a seller who shipped quickly and the product was as advertised. For a seller who made some minor mistakes, but everything came out OK in the end. For a seller who messed up, but was willing to make it right in the end. For an honest seller who did their best to correct a bad situation. For a buyer who left positive feedback. Before leaving this feedback, ask yourself, "If I see this eBay member again, would I trust him?" If the answer is yes and you think he is basically honest then positive feedback is appropriate.

Neutral Feedback – If the seller tried to make things right then leave positive feedback. If the seller made things right but only after giving you the run-around, then Neutral may be appropriate. Neutral Feedback is not counted against the recipient in the totals, but members do not make any distinction between Neutral or Negative when reading comments.

Negative Feedback – For a seller who was intentionally deceptive and unwilling to correct the situation. For a seller who does not respond to Message Console messages. For a seller who does not ship the goods(not lost in the mail but never shipped). For the seller who was incompetent and hard to deal with or had a bad attitude.

<u>username12345</u>(0) 🔒   Having a zero feedback rating is like wearing a sign saying **"I'm new". Many sellers do not trust zero feedback buyers because they are often scammers or inexperienced users who may not pay for what they buy.**

Make The Most of Feedback

Now that you know how feedback works and how important it is in determining the legitimacy of a buyer or seller, let's see how we can make the most of our feedback.

After you have created your new account look closely. We have the dreaded zero feedback rating.

You should never setup an account and immediately begin trying to sell. Smart buyers do not trust sellers with zero feedback. Zero feedback sellers are frequently frauds. Legitimate sellers always buy items to gain experience and become comfortable using eBay. No legitimate seller sets up an account and immediately posts a professional looking auction for an expensive item. Anyone who has zero feedback and has a nice looking auction clearly has auction experience and has setup a new account. Why does someone need to setup a new account? They do it to escape negative feedback or because their old account was disabled due to fraud. Some dishonest sellers and buyers do this routinely. They commit fraud several times until their feedback is negative, then they abandon that account and create a new account. This is why buyers and sellers should not trust zero feedback people.

Now how do we gain feedback if no one trusts us? Simple. We start small. It is against eBay rules to buy or sell feedback, but there are many inexpensive items on eBay that can be purchased which will result in the legitimate exchange of positive feedback. You can find items that have 'Buy-It-Now' options. Buy-It-Now allows you to pay a fixed price instead of bidding and waiting until the end of the auction. Buy items that you normally would purchase locally or through mail order. You can frequently find these at lower prices on eBay. When you need a razor, check eBay. If you want a music CD, check eBay first. The children want a certain new toy? Order it on eBay. Every time you buy through eBay you have an opportunity to increase your feedback.

Inexperienced eBay'ers often recommend looking look for inexpensive one cent or 99 cent items that are either not shipped like downloadable ebooks and using the Buy-It-Now option to purchase them. Be warned, eBay knows about the one cent eBooks. This is a common cover for selling feedback. It is quite obvious that no one would sell an item for a total cost that is less than what they paid to list the item. Never bid on any low priced auction where the seller promises positive feedback. EBay may cancel the sellers account and the buyers account if they suspect it is actually a feedback exchange and not a legitimate sale. Make legitimate purchases and not token feedback purchases. You do not want to build your feedback with several low priced items. This is how scammers build their feedback and you do not want your account to look like a scammer's account. Make legitimate purchases and your feedback will build naturally. Never try to inflate it with low priced purchases. You should neither buy nor sell items that may appear to be a cover for selling feedback. Experienced bidders will easily spot this pattern in your profile.

Inexperienced buyers may never look at your feedback except to glance at the number and maybe the percentage. These members will always bid. They will even bid on sellers with negative feedback. Experienced buyers will look more closely. The experienced buyers are the ones who will pay top prices for your auctions. When I say pay, I mean pay, not just bid. They will actually pay and not walk away sticking the seller with the listing fees. Inexperienced users who bid high prices without looking at the sellers feedback may not pay.

After you use Buy-It-Now, immediately use your PayPal account to pay. Then when you have received your item, leave positive feedback for the seller. They will reciprocate by leaving you positive feedback. It is easy to buy items you really do need on eBay to build your feedback.

You can email a nice message saying you enjoyed the product and left the seller positive feedback and you hope they can do the same for you. After several of these purchases you will have more experience buying on eBay and you will have established that you are trustworthy which is shown by your increased feedback rating. Every person who leaves you positive feedback increases your feedback rating by one. Every person who leaves negative feedback decreases it by one.

Build your feedback to at least 10 before trying to sell anything. Start off selling inexpensive items. Buyers will have less trust for a seller with low feedback and especially for a seller who has previously only had feedback from buying items. There is no need to wait until your feedback is higher. If you are interested in selling, start building your seller feedback now. You do not want to sell 99 cent items. Sell real items that cost under $50. This will give you experience using eBay and build buyers trust in you. You should not build your feedback up with 10 buys in a short period and then offer a $1000 computer laptop. Experienced bidders will not trust you when they see a low feedback score which is only for bought items. You need to establish yourself as a seller before you can successfully sell higher priced items. If you try to sell high priced items without a feedback rating that shows you are a trustworthy seller, you will either not sell the items or you will receive lower bids placed by inexperienced members or thrill bidders who may not pay. You may also attract fraudulent bidders who are looking for inexperienced sellers to take advantage of. Build some feedback and experience buying. Then begin selling inexpensive items to gain experience as a seller. You will soon have a feedback rating of 50 or more and buyers will trust you much more when they see you have a history of positive seller experience.

As a seller, you should never leave feedback first. There are sellers who immediately leave positive feedback when payment is received. I do not believe this is a good practice. You do not know if the transaction will go well or not. If you leave positive feedback immediately then you may be rewarding a problem or dishonest buyer. What if the buyer files a false chargeback through PayPal or claims the item was not as described when it was or leaves you negative feedback without attempting to resolve the situation? If you have already left positive feedback then you cannot remove it and you have rewarded a dishonest buyer. Sellers should only give positive feedback in return for receiving positive feedback. If you leave the buyer positive feedback he has little incentive to leave you positive feedback. When a seller leaves positive feedback first, the buyer is much more likely to leave negative feedback if he has a problem instead of attempting to resolve the problem(this is because many buyers do not know sellers cannot leave negative feedback anymore). If the buyer thinks he could receive negative feedback in response, he will be more likely to contact the seller to resolve a problem before leaving negative feedback.

It is the buyer's responsibility to leave feedback first. Only the buyer can close the transaction with feedback. The seller has no way of knowing whether the transaction

> *Many sellers and buyers do not leave feedback. Some are lazy and do not bother, some do not understand the system and some are afraid to leave negative feedback even when it is deserved. You can check a 'recent feedback' history for any seller to see if they leave feedback or not. This tab is available on the seller's feedback page. You may not want to buy from a discourteous seller who never leaves feedback.*

was good or not until the buyer leaves feedback. If the seller leaves positive feedback immediately or when receiving payment, he may find out later the buyer was a dishonest buyer who demands a refund and wants to keep the goods too.

The buyer must receive the goods and OK the transaction by leaving positive feedback if it went well. The seller should then leave positive feedback in return.

If you sell an item and a buyer demands you leave them feedback, DO NOT DO IT! This is a trick by dishonest buyers. They want to trick you into leaving them positive feedback so they can leave you negative feedback without worry of receiving negative feedback themselves. Once you leave feedback, you cannot change it. Beware of anyone who demands you leave feedback for them first. If you buy an item and the seller sends an email demanding you leave feedback, DO NOT DO IT! There is something wrong with any seller who demands feedback. The seller may be a scammer trying to build feedback so they can scam others. Beware of anyone, buyer or seller, who demands you leave them feedback.

There will always be some people who leave negative feedback for the thrill of it, but the majority of eBay users are honest and will leave truthful feedback.

You can easily avoid this trap as a seller by never leaving feedback for buyers first and always filing unpaid item complaints for buyers who do not pay. It is a waste of the seller's time to leave feedback for everyone because many people will never reciprocate feedback once they have their positive feedback.

When you are the buyer, you should leave feedback when you receive the item and are satisfied the item is as described.

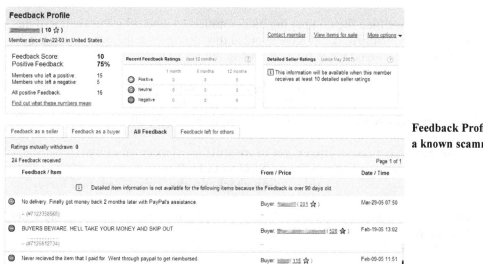

Feedback Profile for a known scammer.

There are many ways to receive negative feedback as a seller:

Ways to receive negative feedback as a seller

- **Charge $12 shipping and then ship the item by first class for $0.75**
- **Wait a week before shipping an item.**
- **Fail to ship an item**
- **Show an auction photo of the perfect right side of an item, but not the damaged left side.**
- **Poorly package an item which results in it being damaged during shipping.**
- **The shipping company loses the package and the buyer never receives the item.**
- **The buyer gives a bogus shipping address and never receives item.**
- **Customs loses the package so the buyer never receives the item.**

Ways to receive negative feedback as a buyer

- **No longer possible under eBay rules.**

You can respond to feedback that has been left for you. This will add a comment below the feedback to give your side of the story. On your MyEBay page you can view your feedback and post a one line response by clicking the Feedback Forum link. If a buyer leaves negative feedback saying "Never received item" and you know the buyer never paid for the item, you should file an Unpaid Item Notification and post a response letting viewers of your feedback know the person never paid. This is what the seller's feedback profile might look like.

> From Buyer: **(-)"Never received the golf club"**
> **Response From Seller: "Buyer never paid for auction"**

The seller should have filed the non paying bidder notice 10 days after the auction if he had not received payment. He could have avoided this attack from the non paying bidder or had the feedback removed when the non-paying bidder case was completed.

You can also post a follow-up comment in the other person's feedback listing. This is what the buyer's feedback might look like once the seller has posted positive feedback which he now realizes he should not have done and follow-up feedback.

> From Seller: **(+) Great Buyer, get more stuff from xxxx on eBay.**
> **Follow-up From Seller: "NEGATIVE: Buyer**
> **said sending check, no check received, bad buyer"**

This situation would have been avoided if the buyer had paid using PayPal and the seller had waited before leaving positive feedback.

Feedback is not a way to communicate with the buyer or seller. It is a final rating to let other members know how the transaction went. If a buyer or seller has a problem, he should contact the other party directly through the eBay Message Center. Feedback should not be made until the transaction is completed or cancelled. Once you submit feedback, it cannot be easily changed.

Here is an example of neutral feedback I saw in an actual seller's profile:

(N) Item has not been sent so feedback will be delayed. ebayusername123(1)

If the buyer had a problem, he should have contacted the seller and not posted neutral feedback. This was completely unfair. Feedback is not for communicating with the seller. The item could have been lost by the shipper or the buyer may not have sent payment. Now that the buyer has left undeserved feedback he cannot leave feedback again or change it easily.

Stick to the facts when leaving feedback. It is not a place for emotional outcries. It is not the place to explain everything in detail. What happened, what was the result.

Libel laws do apply. If a member makes false statements, the other member can sue the person who posted false or libelous statements.

Game came finally! Thank you!	Buyer: ali...tti (133 ☆)	
ROBOTECH INVASION XBOX SHOOTER GAME NEW AND SEALED (#23012713...7)	US $0.01	
I ahve not recieved my item and it has been 3 weeks	Buyer: ...72 (2)	
• Reply by egamesuniverse (May-17-07 08:50): we didn't know you never received game, contact us for reship		
CRASH BANDICOOT 2 PLAYSTATION 1&2 GAME NEW SEALED PS2 (#2301174...3)	US $4.99	
Fast Service Great Description Great Price Great Seller Thanks FANTASTIC PERFECT	Buyer: gabel5004 (36 ☆)	
XBOX 360 NYKO INTERCOOLER FAN COOLING SYSTEM ATTACHMENT (#23012...1)	US $3.99	

Example of unfair and inappropriate negative feedback from an inexperienced user.

> **Good examples of feedback**
> - Slow to ship, but item was well packed, Im happy
> - Nice guy, very polite, received item quickly
> - Item was broken, but seller made it right
> - Fast to ship, but item was broken, seller gave refund so all is OK
> - Great buyer, great communication would do business with again!
> - 2wks after payment and nothing, filed PayPal complaint, no resp to emails
> - Item arrived damaged, seller will not respond to emails, filed ppal complaint
> - Seller backed out, said my bid was too low, but I was high bidder
> - Buyer never paid, ignored payment notices, NPB filed

The above feedback statements tell other members what to expect from this member.

> **Bad examples of feedback**
> - It was ok
> - I got it
> - Seller Sucks
> - u know why this is neutral
> - what a rip off

These feedback statements say more about the intelligence of the person leaving the feedback than they do about the seller. They contain no facts and no information about the actual transaction. They give no useful information to other potential buyers. These are not feedback statements.

When leaving feedback, make sure it is accurate, it is truthful, and make sure it says something meaningful to other eBay members.

Never leave negative feedback without attempting to resolve the matter with the other party first. As a general rule, if you have less than 5 feedbacks, you should not leave negative feedback at all. Many new and inexperienced members leave negative feedback that is undeserved. The members may not understand the system, they may do something incorrectly, or they may have unrealistic expectations for quality or delivery of an item. Wait until you have some experience before considering leaving negative feedback for another member.

Think twice about leaving negative feedback if someone has a lot of positive feedback listings. Your feedback may be deserved and if so it should be posted. If your experience is far out of the norm when compared to other buyers, maybe there was a misunderstanding.

If a seller has a lot of positive feedback, but you have clearly become the victim of fraud, ask yourself if this account has been hijacked(taken over by a criminal who obtained the password). The actual account owner may not be the person you have dealt with.

You can easily leave feedback up to 90 days after an auction ends. After 90 days, the auction is removed from eBay. You will need the auction number(saved in your emails) to leave feedback after that time.

Buyers and sellers should focus on making sales or buying what you want and not building feedback. Don't think of your feedback rating as a rating of you as a person. Feedback is not the purpose of having an eBay account.

EBay 'may' remove feedback if
- **It receives a court order or appropriate court papers**
- **Both parties agree to mutually withdraw the feedback**
- **The feedback is not related to the transaction on eBay**
- **The feedback contains a website url or a script**
- **The feedback contains racist, vulgar or profane language**
- **The feedback contains personally identifiable information like a phone number**
- **The feedback implies there is an investigation by eBay or law enforcement**
- **The feedback is left by a user who supplied fraudulent information during registration**
- **The feedback was left by someone who is No Longer A Registered User**
- **The feedback was left by an ineligible member or minor**
- **The feedback was intentional harassment**
- **The feedback was intended for another user**

What does this removal policy actually mean? Let's take a closer look at each element.

- **eBay receives court papers showing the disputed feedback is slanderous, libelous, defamatory or otherwise illegal**

This requires an actual court order. You would have to hire a lawyer and file a court case. The court would have to find in your favor and agree that the feedback was slanderous, libelous, or defamatory.

- **Both parties agree to mutually withdraw the feedback**

This is the new Mutual Withdrawal feature. If both parties agree the dispute is settled, then the rating is removed but the comment remains. This only requires the members to mutually agree to the removal

- **The feedback contains racist, vulgar or profane language**

This is self explanatory. Feedback calling the member a scam-artist is not covered here.

- **The feedback contains personally identifiable information like a phone number**

If the feedback has your first or last name and it is not part of your eBay ID, the feedback may be removable. Any feedback with your address, phone or email would be removable too. It is interesting to note that someone can leave their own personal information in a feedback comment, but not the other party's.

- **The feedback implies there is an investigation by eBay or law enforcement**

This one is very clear and many feedback remarks have been removed because of hot headed buyers or sellers leaving such feedback. The comment does have to be very specific such as *"the police are investigating this scammer"* or *"I have opened both paypal and ebay investigations for this seller"*.

- **The feedback contains a website url or a script**

Feedback may not contain any reference to a website including elements clearly meant to be a url such as "he is a *scammer for details see nopaypal dot com*". No code such as java script is allowed in html comments.

- **The feedback was intended for another user**

The full text is: *Negative feedback intended for another member will be considered for removal only in situations where the member responsible for the mistaken posting informs eBay of the error and has already placed the same feedback for the correct member.*

This requires the cooperation of both parties and eBay. You will have more success using the Mutual Withdrawal form.

- **The feedback was left by an ineligible member or minor**

Ineligible members are unable to leave feedback anyway. Those who obtain accounts fraudulently, by lying about their personal information or claiming to be adults who are actually minors are unenforceable. It is not eBay's responsibility to prove the person was a minor or provided false information even if it is obvious. The recipient of the negative feedback must be the one to prove it.

- **The feedback is left by a user who supplied fraudulent information during registration**

This is completely at eBay's discretion. If their phone number works then there is no way to prove it is not a valid number unless it is a fax only line. If the person does not respond to their email, then the member may have the feedback removed. A member who is using an abandoned or disabled email(spammer accounts are frequently disabled) will not respond to an eBay verification and you 'may' be able to have scammer comments removed.

- **The feedback was intentional harassment**

This means another member purchased an item, or even created an account, soley for the purpose of leaving negative feedback. If a member bids or uses Buy-It-Now and immediately leaves bad feedback, eBay 'may' remove their comment. It depends on who is reviewing the case and how they interpret the feedback comment. All you have to do is prove it was harassment.

- **The feedback was left by someone who is No Longer A Registered User**

This policy has a lot of power. EBay does not want members, who are such bad apples that their accounts are disabled, to affect the accounts of others. Watch your feedback closely and if a member changes to No Longer Registered within 90 days of the transaction, you can file for a removal. This is supposed to be automatic, but it may not always happen automatically and not every suspended user qualifies to have their comments removed from other member's profiles. If a member can resolve the issue and become reinstated at a later date, their comments will not be removed. This can happen if the member's account was disabled because of non-payment of eBay fees. If a scammer has left you negative feedback and you see their account is disabled soon afterwards, make sure you request their feedback be removed if it is not automatically removed. This policy is another reason it is important to report policy violations, non-paying bidders, and other infractions to eBay. If enough people report an infraction, the person who left undeserved negative feedback may have their account disabled and everyone they left feedback for in the past 90 days will have it removed.

It is not against eBay policy to lie in feedback as long as it does not go so far as to break the law.

Mutual Withdrawal

There is a better option for removing feedback. If both parties agree, they can select the Mutual Withdrawal option. You can find a shortcut to the Mutual Withdrawal page at http://portal.dont-bid-on-it.com. On this page, both members can enter the auction item number and agree to have their ratings removed. The comments will remain, but the negative, neutral, or positive rating will no longer be shown and will not count in either parties percentage rating. This system is supposed to allow members to remove feedback after a disagreement has been resolved. Unfortunately, this system now encourages retaliatory feedback. If one member leaves legitimate negative feedback, the other member will often leave retaliatory negative feedback hoping the victim will agree to Mutual Withdrawal.

There is no fee and the process is automatic once both parties file the Mutual Feedback form. You can file for Mutual Withdrawal even if one party has not left feedback. Mutual Withdrawal will make it impossible for the other party to leave feedback for the transaction if they have not already done so.

Responding To Feedback

If someone leaves positive or neutral feedback in your profile that says something negative or bad, you do not want to post a follow-up response.

(+) Fast to ship but product was broken, would not recommend

A follow-up response will only draw attention to the comment. Members do not read positive rated comments, only negative or neutral comments. The comment will soon be pushed onto later pages as you add more positive feedback ratings. There is no need to highlight it with a comment. A neutral rating will not count against your overall rating anyway and after twelve months it will not even show up in your profile summary.

READING FEEDBACK

When you see negative feedback in someone's profile, check the profile of the person who left the negative feedback. Look at the person's own profile. Does he have lots of negatives himself? Check his feedback-left-for-others history. Does he have a habit of leaving negative feedback? Any member who has left more than one negative comment for every 100 transactions likely IS the problem member. If a person has problems in more than 1 in 100 transactions, then that person is either a problem member or is choosing to buy from shady auctions. It is not normal for an honest member to leave negative feedback on a regular basis.

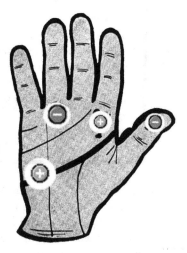

Reading feedback is more complicated than simply looking at the positive percentage or the last few ratings.

If a buyer leaves negative feedback for a seller claiming they were 'ripped off' it does not necessarily make the claim true. You should look for other feedback in both profiles and see if either party has a history of similar complaints. One negative among many positives is not an indication of a dishonest buyer or seller. A single negative may be a transaction that simply went bad or a problem member with limited experience.

Also compare the overall ratings. A seller with 2 negatives and 1000 positives is more believable than a buyer with three positive ratings over his entire eBay lifetime.

Check the 'feedback left for others' tab on any member you do business with. Does the buyer have a history of defending themselves against non-payment? Does the buyer have a history of buying bad items? It is unusual for a buyer to have a problem with every purchase. Any buyer who has a habit of posting negative feedback is either a buyer who is impossible to please, has unrealistic expectations, or simply likes to leave negative feedback for others. You can usually compare the comments to determine if this buyer is leaving honest feedback or just posting negative feedback because he can.

If a seller has a history of good feedback, but his last five or ten feedbacks are negatives from different people, this usually means the account was compromised. A scammer has obtained the password and is using the account to commit fraud. Never buy from a seller who has a series of recent negatives from different buyers. Report the account to eBay as a suspected hijacked account.

I avoid sellers who have a number of comments, positive or negative, that say they do not respond to emails. I do not like dealing with sellers who ignore customer emails. If you have a problem they will not respond.

Half of all buyers will leave feedback to receive positive feedback in return, the other half never leave feedback. You can estimate that every positive rating generally represents two positive experiences and each negative rating represents up to three negative experiences. This rule only applies if the member has multiple negative ratings. If they only have one or two negatives among two hundred or more positives, those can usually be ignored.

If someone has a rating of +5 which consists of eight positive and three negative, it actually indicates they have up to 9 negative experiences to 16 positive experiences. This will help you to determine how trustworthy someone is. If I saw a seller with that rating, I would not buy from him.

Some buyers are unreasonable. They will order a product then leave negative feedback for the seller if the delivery service smashed the box. The damage has nothing to do with the seller because he did nothing wrong, but some buyers will still leave undeserved negative feedback. This is one of the risks of doing business with other people. I have actually had buyers use buy-now on a Sunday night then complain that they had not received their purchase on Monday morning.

Some buyers may buy a book or music CD and then leave the seller negative feedback if they did not like the music or thought the book was boring. The seller had nothing to do with writing the book or recording the music. It is unfair for a buyer to leave such feedback, but they often do. I ignore such buyer negative comments when I see them in a seller's profile. Those are problems with the buyer, not the seller.

Certain products, like open box items or used laptops, generate negative feedback more often or may attract people who are more likely to leave negative feedback. This will cause sellers of high dissatisfaction items to have more negative feedback than other sellers.

Sellers with many thousands of ratings will frequently have more negative feedback ratings. A seller who sells hundreds or thousands of products a week will be less capable of responding to customer concerns and is more likely to make shipping mistakes which can generate negative feedback. High volume sellers also deal with many people so they will also deal with more problem buyers. This can result in more negative feedback comments which does not necessarily mean they are bad sellers.

Large sellers often sell store returns or refurbished merchandise. These can generate negative feedback because buyers do not read the entire auction and are upset when they receive an open box item. Used laptop computers are commonly sold with bad batteries. This is stated in the listings. Buyers often do not read the complete listing then leave undeserved negative feedback saying the battery is bad. The problem was that the buyer did not read the auction before bidding.

You should always check a seller's feedback to see if their negatives are deserved or not. My rule is if I have trouble finding their negative feedback, they must be pretty good. If they do have negative feedback and the comments are nonsense, then I dismiss them as bad buyers.

Feedback can reveal the true nature of a buyer or seller. It is important to leave feedback after every transaction and even more important to check it before placing a bid.

Part IV Selling

Chapter 12 - Selling 101

Once you are comfortable buying on eBay, you will be ready to sell. Everyone has some extra items around the house they would like to turn into cash. EBay is the place to make some money from those old, unused items.

Seller Systems

In order to change potential buyers into actual buyers, you need a system that will help them make that buying decision. This is where most sellers fail. They throw an item on eBay and hope it sells high. They do not understand what an auction needs to be successful. It can be as simple as putting the right kind of photo in your listing, or answering a question in your listing that every buyer will want to know the answer to. The most important elements of an auction are the easiest to include.

Unfortunately many sellers, even experienced sellers, have no system. Many sellers mistakenly believe they are successful because they have feedback ratings of 1000 or more. They do not realize they are making basic mistakes that are costing them money on every item they sell. Sellers may start offering items with a dream of making eBay their full time business and quickly fail. They list items which either do not sell or sell at low prices (which is good for the smart buyers) and give up, then blame eBay for their failure. EBay is just a listing location, no different from setting up a booth at a flea market. It is up to the seller to make their listing appeal to buyers. Making your listing appeal to buyers is very easy, if you know the basics.

There are many coffee makers being offered on eBay, but almost none are actually selling unless they are high end espresso machines or rare collector's items. No one cares about buying a cheap coffee machine on eBay when they can pick one up locally for less than it would cost to ship. Sell an item that people will want to buy.

What are we selling?

We need to know what item we are selling, what category it goes in, and at what price we should set our opening bid.

First we need to pick something to sell. The majority of items on eBay are smaller items. There are people selling washers and dryers, but those items are not easy for the average person to ship. You may find someone willing to pickup locally if you are in a large city, but large items are not usually practical to sell.

Some exceptions to the large item shipping rule are vehicles, arcade games and antique furniture. These are expensive items so people will pay to ship them. Items that are valuable enough to justify the shipping expense can be good sellers.

Small items, under 45 pounds, that will fit in a medium to large size box are the best items to sell. These can be easily packaged and shipped by the average person.

What is it worth?

Pick something to sell that has value.

Some items are too inexpensive to bother selling. If your initial research shows that there are thousands of auctions for a regular deck of playing cards and almost none are closing with bidders, then don't bother trying to sell playing cards unless your item is special or you are selling them by the case.

Some items attract fraud and others rarely see fraudulent transactions. The amount of fraud you see depends heavily on what you sell which determines who you are selling to. Expensive items that can be easily resold are common targets for fraud, such as laptops and new gaming consoles. Items small time criminals want to use for themselves may be targets of fraud such as computer games and computer parts. Your fraud levels will be very low if you buy and sell doll head vases. The people who are interested in doll head vases are less likely to be involved in fraudulent activity.

Timing is Everything

Do we want to sell our item now? We may want to wait if someone else is selling the same item. Don't list a rare Philco Tube Radio if someone else has a listing for the same radio. If you try to sell yours at the same time someone else is selling the same item, it will reduce your profit. Do not post your auction immediately after the other auction for the same item ends. If you can wait a couple of weeks or a month and no other similar items are posted, then you will sell for a higher amount.

You may not want to post your item at all if there are fifty other people selling the same item and these auctions are closing with no bidders. There is no point in offering an item no one wants. Wait a month or more and check the market again.

Some items will not sell as easily at certain times of the year. There is always a market for Halloween costumes, but before Halloween is when you can really make money on them. You will not make nearly as much selling them in January.

> *I saw an opportunity in some Halloween Fortune Tellers. Before Halloween, Sam's Club purchased thousands of these, but they did not send them out to the stores like they should have. As Halloween came closer they decided they had to liquidate them on their website. The price went from $65 each to $19 each. I bought a UPS truck full of them. They sat in storage for a year until the next Halloween. During this time there were many sellers on eBay offering these for $60 then $40 then $20 until they sold out. The market was flooded at that time. I did not sell. I waited. When Halloween came around again, these models were no longer made. Now this was a collectable item in high demand. I began selling them in September for $120 each. That is timing.*

eBay Arbitrage

When a buyer buys an item on eBay, and immediately tries to resell it on eBay, it is called eBay arbitrage. This seldom works because most of the time when an item is re-auctioned, it brings a lower price. If your high bidder fails to pay and you re-auction an item, it will sell at a lower price the second time around. This happens because buyers are tapped out. Their interest is piqued by the auction, their anticipation builds, and when the auction is over, their interest drops. Buyers need time to become interested in another auction for the same item. One exception to this rule is for high demand items which usually have steady values and lots of buyers.

You should not attempt to sell an item before the item is in your hands. It could be lost, not shipped, or have damage you did not know about.

WHAT IS IT?

What is the item? This may sound silly, but many people try to sell items on eBay without knowing the name of the item or even knowing what it is used for. If you do not know, you should try to find something that describes it so people can find your listing by keywords. The title must accurately describe the item. If it is unclear or incomplete, you will receive a lower price or no bids at all.

CATEGORY

What category should the item go under? The obvious category may not be the correct or best category. Sometimes collectors as a group lay claim to a category and that becomes '*their*' category where they buy and sell. This may not be the category you would expect. Search for similar items and see where other people are listing them.

You want your category to be as specific as possible. This means continuing through the category selection options until you hit the bottom and no more options appear. For instance, you do not want to list an item under the Bath category. That category has thousands of items in it and many sub categories. No one will every look through the Bath category to find your item. Viewers will look in specific categories for specific types of items. Imagine trying to find an item in the encyclopedia if it is '*somewhere*' in the encyclopedia versus listing the item in the correct book, in the correct section, the correct page along with other similar topics. Members can find your item when it is listed in the correct sub category. They may never see it when it is listed in a higher category.

There are many categories on eBay and your item may fit in two or more. When you research similar auctions, you will see where other people are listing their items. Then you will know which category to use. You can list your item in more than one category, but the listing fees are doubled.

ODD CATEGORY LISTINGS

List your item in the correct category. Some sellers think they will receive more bids by listing their item in popular categories instead of the correct category. This will not only cause an item to receive lower bids, it can trigger an eBay complaint for miscategorizing auctions.

There are many categories with close followers who take offense when a seller spams their group with items not related to it. If you see an item that is clearly and intentionally miscategorized, you should report it to eBay using the Report This Listing link.

Honest sellers do not post items in inappropriate groups. Smart buyers know this. When a seller posts an item in a group that is not related to the item, buyers will not trust the seller. They should not. The seller has already resorted to deceptive and dishonest tactics to make people look at his auction.

> *There was a less than honest seller who would cross post his Japanese swords in the arcade game categories. The swords had nothing to do with the categories he was posting in, but the seller thought he could spam the groups with his auctions and gain more sales. He did not have to compete with other sellers offering similar swords in the appropriate categories. Intentionally listing items in unrelated categories is rude and inconsiderate of the people who watch that category. Watchers of the arcade categories filed complaints and his auctions were cancelled. I never would have purchased from this seller even if I were interested in a Japanese sword. Honest sellers list their items in the correct groups.*

TITLE KEYWORDS

Choose your title keywords very carefully.

The majority of items on eBay are found based on keywords in the title.
Buyers enter keywords in the search box to search auction titles.

Words such as "prohibited", "banned", "illegal", "outlawed" or similar words that imply the item may be illegal are not allowed. These words themselves are not banned. If your item is a book about 'illegal immigration' that is an acceptable use of the word. If your item is a 'Radar Jammer, illegal in most states' that is a violation of eBay rules.

SPAMMING KEYWORDS

You want your title to be clear and to contain important key words. The title should not be too wordy. Never spam the title with lots of keywords designed to make the listing appear for any search or unrelated searches.

Lawnmower, mow lawns, fun, computer, video game, antique

The seller using the above title is trying to include a lot of unnecessary and non-descriptive words to make their auction appear for searches that are not related to the item. If he is trying to sell a lawnmower then why does he have 'video game' and 'antique' in the description? He is trying to make his listing appear when people search for other items. This is a dishonest tactic and is called keyword spamming. Such sellers do not receive more bids; they receive fewer because buyers do not trust them. Never trust a seller who resorts to dishonest tactics to trick people into looking at their auction.

Example of a good title
Toro 5200D fairway Lawn Mower Lawnmower

Notice that I used both lawnmower and lawn mower as two words because a potential bidder may type either one in the search box. I want to make sure that no matter what they type, they find my auction listing. I included the manufacturer and the model number. If someone is looking for this specific model, they will find my auction with a simple search. If I did not include this information, interested searchers may never see my auction.

Example of bad auction titles
Lawnmower for sale -no information, no keywords, and for sale is meaningless in an auction
Lwanmower cheep – misspelled words
Toro, used – not enough information and no keywords
TORO LAWNMOWER – no information, titles should not be all CAPS

Ask yourself, "*If I were looking to buy this exact item, what would I search for to find it.*" Those are your keywords.

Avoid words like '*fun*', '*funky*' or '*nostalgia*' in the title. Even if it is accurate, it can be considered spamming if it is not part of the item name. Your auction could be cancelled by eBay if they think you are spamming your title keywords. It is appropriate to list a word like vintage. There are thousands of radios on eBay. If your radio is a vintage radio, then you should say so in the title. **Vintage Philco Tube Radio**. Anyone looking for a vintage radio and not specifically a Philco can find your listing out of the thousands of new and old radio listings.

Titles cannot include brand names that do not represent the item being sold. An auction with a title like "**XYZ Jeans, just like Ralph Lauren**" is a violation of eBay rules because Ralph Lauren jeans are not being sold in the auction. Using unnecessary words, unrelated brand names, or words meant to appear in unrelated searches is keyword spamming and that is a violation of eBay rules.

Stick to basic letters and numbers with minimum punctuation.
Vintage Philco Tube Radio 1928 - is appropriate
Vintage Philco Tube Radio 1928 L@@K!!!! - is not appropriate

No one searches for L@@K and it makes the title look cluttered. Many buyers are put off by such attempts to draw their attention and may see the seller as a '*wheeler and dealer*' instead of an honest seller.

Do not use words like WOW or LOOK in the title. Those are not search terms. EBay requires that titles describe the item being offered.

Only use abbreviations in the title if you expect buyers to search on those abbreviations.

SUBTITLES

Use all of the appropriate keywords in your title. You can pay extra for a subtitle, but subtitle words will not be searched in a keyword search. Put your important keywords in the main title. Subtitles are better used for a hook, like 'Use Buy-It-Now and Get Free Shipping' or 'Includes all accessories'. This extra note can make your item more interesting among a crowd of similar items.

Genco Sky Gunner 1953 EM Game
rebuilt and working like new

Subtitles are not searched for keywords.

IT'S RARE! REALLY! TRUST ME!

Never call your item rare or collectable in the title. It is offensive to collectors who know what is rare and what is not. Experts often do not appreciate being told something is rare. Beginners will be more skeptical when they see a seller claiming something is rare. Beginners think if the seller has to say it is rare then maybe it is not rare, but a sales pitch.

Don't call an item Rare in the title or description. It puts off both experienced and beginner collectors. It is OK to say you have a special rare version in the description if you also say why it is a rare version, "This is a special color that was only produced in 1955."

"This is the rare black color which makes it very collectable."

LOCATION

The item information box shows where the item is located. This is important information and should be accurate. Saying the item is 'In The USA' will not help sales, it will hurt sales. In the USA could mean anywhere. Some buyers like to buy from local sellers and choose the closest seller even if the item is being shipped. Some large items may need to be picked up and the buyer will want to know where the item is located before they bid. This information does not have to be exact and should not be a street address. A simple statement of the city, state, country is enough. This helps buyers estimate arrival time. Some sellers use cute sayings or generic locations. This is a mistake and it makes buyers mistrust the seller. Buyers do not trust sellers who hide where they are located.

Starting bid:	US $1,100.00 [Place Bid >]
Buy It Now price:	US $1,300.00 [Buy It Now >]
End time:	Apr-30-07 22:19:38 PDT (6 days 22 hours)
Shipping costs:	US $350.00 Standard Flat Rate Shipping Service Service to United States
Ships to:	United States
Item location:	houston, TX, United States
History:	0 bids

Good location:
   Houston TX, USA
   San Francisco CA, Sunset District

Bad location:
   The Great USA
   SALE SPECIALS EVERY DAY
   A Town Near You
   Worldwide Shipping

Left, top of auction with location as Houston TX, United States. Above, good and bad examples

The location area is not a place to make sales pitches, describe shipping or terms, and certainly not the place to list cryptic messages. List your city, state, country in the location box. A seller who does not list a real location appears to be trying to hide. This will make buyers distrust the seller and result in lower bids or fewer bidders.

AUCTION LENGTH

How long should an auction last? We want to list our auction so the most people see it. Page views go up on Saturday and Sunday. This tells you that you should run auctions for the 7 day period through a weekend. If you can end late on a Sunday evening, that is perfect for collectables because you have the most weekend page views plus the fact that your auction is ending during a high page view time and will show up in the category listing for 'ending-soonest'. This greatly increases the number of people who see your auction. You may not want to list your auction to end on Sunday evening if you have a lot of competition or sell a new product. If 100 other sellers are offering the same item and their auctions all close on Sunday, don't bother listing your item to end at the same time. The idea behind ending an auction Sunday evening is well known and many sellers use it. If you have lots of competition on eBay, then Sunday may be the worst time to end an auction because you are competing with other sellers who are ending their auctions during high page-view periods. The Sunday night close only applies to collectables. New items usually see better closing prices during the week.

Auctions that end on Monday morning are also good because people who come to work on Monday often check eBay to avoid starting work. They will search and bid on items when they first arrive at work in that 7am to 10am Eastern Time period(4am-7am Pacific). Auctions ending in the evening catch people coming home from work in the 6 P.M. to 11 P.M. Eastern Time (3-8 P.M. Pacific Time) and surfing eBay to relax. After 11 P.M. Eastern Time, your auction will be mostly seen by West Coast viewers until midnight Pacific

Categories on eBay are sorted based on time ending soonest and newly listed.

When your auction is first listed and when it is about to end are the times most people will see it in the category view. The rest of the time, members will see your auction when they search based on the keywords.

Auctions end at the same time they are listed, seven days later. If you list your auctions in the prime times, they will always end in the prime times. You can schedule an auction ending for an additional fee.

During a three day or holiday weekend, many people are away from their computer and may not see your auction. This is not to say you should never list your auctions to end over a 3 day weekend. Many sellers follow that advice and that may leave your auctions as the only ones listed while your competitors take the weekend off.

The US is the biggest market on eBay, but it is not the only market. People in the US may be enjoying a holiday weekend but it will be business as usual in Europe and Canada as well as the rest of the world. If you have a lot of international sales, a holiday may not make much difference in your sales. Not everyone in the US observes holidays.

Generally, if you have an item that depends on emotional bidding wars or an impulse buy item, you want your item to end during the prime times. If you have a new item that is not likely to generate a bidding frenzy, or that attracts experienced bidders, they will use snipe software. The end time is less important because their bid is placed automatically.

Does this really work? It does sometimes and for some items. It does not work for everything. EBay has a worldwide audience so it is always the middle of the day somewhere. It is true that many people are away from home on a three day weekend, but it is also true that many stay home and relax. Shut-in's and the elderly are less likely to vacation away from home and if that is your customer base, your auctions will not be affected by the holiday weekend. There are people who work late or early shifts and can be online at any hour. None of these time rules are absolute.

You have to know your market. Ending Monday, ending Sunday, ending at 2 P.M. Wednesday, there is no magic time. One time may work for one item and not for another, it may work for one seller and not another, it may work for one month and not another. The bottom line is, there are a lot of people on eBay and they will find your item if you follow my listing advice. Post a seven day auction that runs through a weekend and try to end in the morning or evening. Don't worry about perfect timing.

I list my auctions when I list them and they end when they end. I use the 7 day format and I never worry about the exact time. I know the amateur bidders will bid when they see my listing and serious snipe bidders will go for my collectible items using snipe software so the auction end time does not matter. My auctions do not depend on emotional bidding wars so timing is not as critical.

Auctions longer than seven days do not perform better and you have to pay more for them. Shorter auctions do not attract enough bidders. Single day auctions are often used by dishonest sellers trying to make a sale and collect the money before eBay can cancel the auction. A seven day auction will last through a weekend and that is important. Ten day auctions are too long. Many bidders are unwilling to wait for a 10 day auction to end when they can find other auctions ending sooner. Always choose the 7 day auction.

PRICE

Price research is the same as when buying an item. See the Buying section for price research searches. Check past auctions, retail prices, and know your market.

What price should we charge? We can set a fixed price, called a Buy-It-Now price or we can set an opening bid or both. By setting an opening bid we allow bidders to compete for the item. The bidder who places the highest bid is the winner. If you do not know the value of your item or its value is determined by the market, such as antiques or collectables, you should use the auction format.

Sellers sometimes start auctions at $1. They do this to encourage emotional bidding. People see an item for $1 and bid just for the chance at winning something for $1. Then someone bids $2 and $3 and so on. The seller wants to create a bidding frenzy and run the price up. Maybe the end price will be higher than the value of the item. This can work on items that will have lots of bidders, but it can be dangerous on low demand items. A seller may start at $1 and seven days later find that their $500 game console closed at $100.00 with 17 bids. If the seller is not willing to sell at that low of a price, it is too late. They are already obligated to sell to the high bidder who bid in good faith.

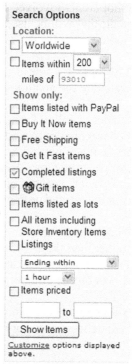

If you post an item at $1 then you must accept the risk that it may not make as much as you had hoped. If you check previous auctions and see a similar item started at $1 and sold for $500, that does not mean that your item will do the same. Every day, every minute is different on eBay. One auction may have many bidders and a day later another auction for the same item may have no bidders at all. I have purchased items on eBay for $100 then sold them a month later for $50. The market changes all the time. The person who was willing to pay $90 last month was gone.

Opening an auction at $1 may result in one bidder buying the item for $1 especially if the item is a specialty item that may not receive many bids anyway. If you are unsure about opening at $1 then set your opening price at the minimum amount you would be willing to take for the item. This is not the dream price you hope someone might pay, it is a realistic bargain basement price.

When comparing the number of bids on similar auctions, look at the opening bid. If two auctions close at $200 and one has 3 bids and the other has 27 bids, I bet the one with 27 bids started at $2.

It is better to list a serious price as your opening bid. Suppose a seller posts a $500 item for $1 then the auction closes for $20 and THEN the seller realize there was an error in the listing which said Model-1 instead of Model-11. Model-1 may be worthless, or worth $20, but it is too late once the auction has closed. If this seller had listed the minimum he was willing to take, then it is likely no one would have bid and he could have relisted with the corrected information. It occasionally happens that an expensive item is listed for $1 and only one bidder bids.

Items that are purchased to be used(not collectables or items for resale) will see higher closing prices if they start with lower opening bids and normal shipping charges. These same items will see lower closing prices if you use a higher opening bid and free shipping.

Bidders look for bargains, especially in new items. Your bidder needs to feel they are receiving a bargain. They may even pay more if they feel it is a bargain.

Bidders want to pay less for an item, but once they perceive it as a bargain, they may continue to bid higher amounts for it. The bidder does not want to 'miss this bargain'. Once a bidder begins bidding for a $4 bargain, they may continue bidding up to $14 even if they never would have considered placing an initial $14 bid. They have become emotionally involved and do not want to lose their bargain. Make your opening bid on items that will be used(non collectables or items not for resale) attractive to bargain hunters.

Low opening bids attract more early bidders which can translate into more people watching the auction until the end.

Bidders think in terms of what they lose, not what they gain when buying new items. Bidders are concerned with losing their money and not as much with gaining the new item. When buying collectables and antiques, they think in terms of what they gain and not what they lose. Bidders want to gain the item and are less concerned about losing the money. This causes bidders to bid more and become more emotionally involved in sales of antiques and collectables.

Make sure your price is reasonable. You cannot set your opening bid higher than retail or higher than the close of other auctions. No one will bid if you do. Make sure your price is not less than you are willing to take unless you are very confident it will be bid up by dream or thrill bidders.

Your choice between a low opening bid or a minimum-you-will-take bid depends on your willingness to accept risk and your confidence in the item's value and demand for the item.

PRICE GUIDES

Price guides are never accurate. You should never price your eBay item based on a price guide. Price guides are just guesses. The California author of a price guide may think an item is very valuable because he never sees the item. A Georgia reader may see the same item sell locally for pennies and think it is worthless. Value depends on who wants the item. Price guides can be out of date before they are printed and completely wrong by the time you buy the book. Professional appraisers cannot tell you 'real' prices. Their prices are based on live auction results or guesswork. I have seen appraisers assign values of $5000 to an item at a live auction that only bid up to $500. It is easy to assign a high value to something when you are not the one writing out the check for it.

The value is what someone is willing to pay for it. The only price for your item is what it sells for. That was its value for the day and time it was sold to the people interested enough to bid on it. That is the only value for the item. An item may sell for $50 on Monday 1 PM, and the same item can sell for $10 on Friday at 7 PM. That is how the market goes sometimes. Past eBay sales are an indicator of what you can expect to receive, but not a guarantee.

PRIVATE AUCTIONS

If you have a valuable item or an item that bidders may not want others to know they are bidding on, you can select a Private Auction. Private auctions hide the bidder's identity. Some collectors of high value or rare items prefer to maintain their privacy. They may not want everyone in their collector community to know they purchased one of three known antique figurines. This is a feature that should only be used in rare cases. Many bidders do not like private auctions and assume the seller has a sinister reason to hide the bidders. Unless there is a clear reason to hide the identities of bidders you should not use this feature. If you do use this feature, you should explain why in the auction. A simple statement can be included such as "This is a private auction where the bidders identity will remain private and will not be visible to other bidders. I understand that this is a rare item of interest to high end collectors and you may not want others to see your identity as a bidder. I will protect your privacy when you bid on my auctions."

If you are selling an item that could be embarrassing for the buyer, then you would have a good reason to use the Private Auction. Bidders would understand why this auction was private and would appreciate the seller's consideration for their privacy.

The item number will be replaced by the word Private in feed back for both parties if they choose to leave feedback. I would suggest not leaving feedback if you really want to keep your purchase private.

Private auctions are commonly used by scammers. They use private auctions to prevent one victim from contacting other victims. They also want to prevent current bidders from contacting bidders on past auctions.

RESERVE PRICES

Never use reserve price auctions. A reserve price is a secret price associated with the auction and if the bidding amount does not meet this secret reserve price, the seller does not have to sell.

Every time I click an auction with a low opening bid price and see the seller has a reserve price, I feel like I have been tricked. I click the back button to find another seller. I do not bid on auctions that have reserve prices if the reserve has not been met by someone else.

After a new eBay member bids on a few reserve price auctions and sees them close with the message 'Reserve Not Met' the bidder loses interest in reserve price auctions. The bidder has learned to avoid these disappointing auctions.

Experienced bidders avoid reserve auctions because even if they are high bidder they do not win. This leaves them feeling cheated by the seller. You want the bidder to feel that they can win you item, not feel like they are about to be cheated.

Reserve prices are usually set too high by the seller. The inexperienced seller is dreaming about what they would like to be paid and not thinking about the value of the item. Reserve prices are usually well above market price. There is no point in bidding on an item if it cannot be won.

Some sellers using reserve prices have no intention of selling the item being offered. They use reserve pricing to determine the market value of the item or to test the waters before actually selling the item. These sellers post an auction and use a reserve price that is many times the value of the item so no one could win the auction. They are rigging the auction. When the auction closes, the seller can look through the high bids and see what everyone bid. Then they decide if they want to make a second chance offer to the high bidder or put the item up for a real auction.

Dishonest sellers may list a very high reserve price and a low opening bid to lure out interested bidders. When the auction ends with no bidders, the seller contacts the bidders and offers to sell the item off of eBay to avoid eBay fees. They may even offer the same item to several people without shipping anything.

Most reserve price auctions close without selling. The seller may have an item worth $300, but he sets the reserve at $500, then opens bidding at $1. The item is bid up to $275 at the auction close which is not over $500 so the seller is not required to sell. None of the bidders knew what the secret price was or they would not have bothered bidding. The seller is wasting the time of all of the bidders.

If the same auction had been run without the reserve price, it might have closed above $300. Bidders were unable to fairly compete without knowing what they were actually bidding against so the high bid was not only less than the reserve, it was less than it might have been without a reserve price. This is also a result of a reduced number of bidders.

Bidders who would have been otherwise interested in the auction did not bid because there was a reserve price.

Reserve Prices can be combined with a Buy-It-Now price. The Buy-It-Now price will remain available even if bids are placed, until the reserve is met. It is not a good idea to use this pricing method. The same problems with Reserve Price auctions still apply. If potential bidders see a reserve and a Buy-It-Now, most will assume the reserve is the same as, or just below the Buy-It-Now price and will not bid unless they are interested in paying the Buy-It-Now price. The seller of this auction would have done better to have offered the item at a fixed price to avoid the stigma of a Reserve Auction.

Using a low reserve price can send the wrong message to bidders. If you set a low reserve amount, it was a mistake to use reserve pricing anyway because eBay charges a reserve price fee. If you do set a low reserve and it is quickly met, the serious bidders who see the auction after the reserve is met will assume the value of the item has been reached. Why should they continue to bid on an item if it has met the value the seller placed on it? They will assume it is already at or over its value and will not bid. If the potential bidders know the value, they may assume there is something wrong with the item if the seller is willing to take less than its actual value as a reserve price and again pass up the auction. Don't give potential bidders reasons to not bid.

Reserve price auctions should never be used. It usually indicates an inexperienced seller. Honest sellers do not have to use secret prices. Reserve pricing drives away bidders. If you are going to sell an item and there is a minimum amount you are willing to take, make that amount your opening bid so everyone can see, don't keep it a secret.

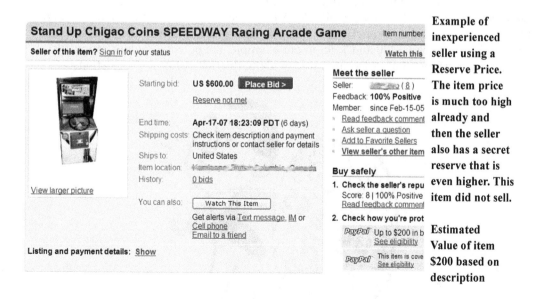

Example of inexperienced seller using a Reserve Price. The item price is much too high already and then the seller also has a secret reserve that is even higher. This item did not sell.

Estimated Value of item $200 based on description

SHOULD YOU USE A BUY-IT-NOW PRICE?

EBay items can be sold as an auction where people bid and the high bidder wins the item or you can set a Buy-It-Now price. The first person willing to pay the buy-it-now price can buy the item as long as no one else has already bid. Buy-it-now is best used when offering items with a known value. Many bidders will pay a premium instead of waiting seven days until the end of the auction. They may also not want to risk losing the auction. The best use of the Buy-It-Now price is to grab the interest of the buyer who is willing to pay extra for it now.

It is always a good idea to give bidders the Buy-It-Now option. Some people do not like to wait 7 days and will pay more to buy now. If there is too much difference between your Buy-It-Now price and your opening bid, a bargain hunter may place a bid and knock out the Buy-It-Now price. This is good if you want to encourage bidding.

If you are selling a collectable, you can set a Buy-It-Now price that is high with a low opening bid. If a buyer finds your auction and is willing to pay extra to be guaranteed the item, they will pay the Buy-It-Now price. If they think the Buy-It-Now price is too high, they can place a bid which will make the Buy-It-Now price unavailable. No one else can use Buy-It-Now once the first bid is placed. You have effectively used a BIN price to encourage an interested person to bid now rather than later.

If you want to sell an item at the fixed price, but not list a fixed price auction and you have an item valued at $200, set the Buy-It-Now at $200 and the opening bid at $195. If you want to encourage bidders to place a bid set the opening bid at $50, someone will bid hoping to win for $50 instead of paying the Buy-It-Now price. The bidder feels pressure to bid now rather than wait and risk someone taking the auction away from them with the Buy-It-Now option. A higher opening bid keeps away these dream-bidders and allows the Buy-It-Now price to remain available. A lower opening bid price encourages bargain hunters to place a bid and knock out the Buy-It-Now price. When the Buy-It-Now and opening bid are close, $200 and $195 in our example, the potential bidder can justify spending a few more dollars to buy it now without the risk of losing the auction.

OTHER LISTING UPGRADES

EBay offers various listing upgrades. EBay makes lots of extra money by charging for these upgrades. Some upgrades are important and some are not. Let's take a look at the important upgrades.

Home Page Featured $39.95

Home Page Featured auctions appear on the eBay main page and cost $39.95 in addition to your listing and final value fees. This is an expensive option and not a good choice for low priced items. I never use this feature. Most members either go to their favorite category or search for a specific item by keywords. The main page takes a lot of hits, but you have to ask yourself whether it is worth the extra cost to be listed there. Will it really gain you a higher price? Most of the time, it will not. Featured listings may help your sales if you have a large number of impulse buy items. I do not recommend using this feature unless you have a compelling reason.

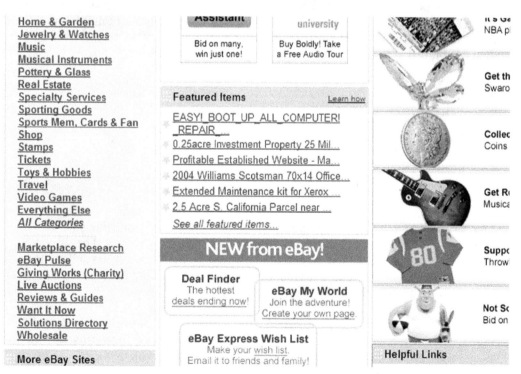

Home Page Featured listings. Can you see them, there in the center? Is it worth $39.95 to show your listing here?

Featured Plus $19.95

Featured Plus listings show up at the top of a category listing or search results. They are separated from regular listings by a gray line. This is a great feature because it keeps your item near the top of the listing during the entire auction. If someone searches for newly listed or about to close auctions, your auction is always near the top no matter how they sort. This means lots of people see your item, not just when it is opening and closing. This feature is not useful in some categories. In popular categories there may be hundreds of people using this feature. Your listing is lost among them. If your category only has a few Featured Plus listings then your item will be seen by every visitor to that category. You would not want to use it for an inexpensive item. I use featured plus when I am offering a multiple item auction for items worth $30 or more or for single items worth over $500. This upgrade is only available to members with a feedback rating of 10 or more.

Gallery Listing $0.35

This option shows a small picture with the auction search listing. This is a must for every auction. You should always use this feature. People shop visually. When someone goes to a mall, they look around, when they see something they like they pick it up to read the box. EBay works the same way. People shop visually. When they see something they like, they read the description. If you have a text only listing among a lot of gallery listings with pictures, potential bidders will never even notice your listing. EBay says a gallery image may increase the final price by 11%*. I think they are wrong. I think it will double the number of people who see your listing and if it makes the difference between an item selling or not, that is a 100% difference. Always use the gallery image feature.

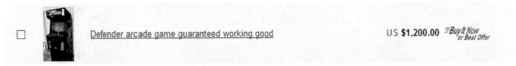

Defender arcade game guaranteed working good   US $1,200.00 =Buy It Now or Best Offer

Gallery Listings show a small image of the item in the search results.

Do not use a logo for your gallery image. You should show the item being sold. Some sellers think they are building a brand by using their logo. They are not. They are losing sales. When a buyer is shopping on eBay they are shopping for items, not sellers. Buyers will ignore a logo and continue browsing for actual photos. Using a logo is worse than a text only listing because the seller paid extra for this feature.

Your gallery image should show the item clearly. Remember that this will be a small image. If your item is not clear or is dark, it may not be visible when the image is smaller. Pick an image for the gallery image that will be clear when shrunk down.

According to eBay, this represents an average based on data from January 2003 transactions.

Gallery Plus $0.75

This option shows your gallery image as a large image when the user mouses over it in the search view and adds an additional option to view "Larger Image". The viewer can see the normal images or the supersize images. . If you need to show details or close-ups, this is a good option. This listing fee is in addition to the Gallery fee.

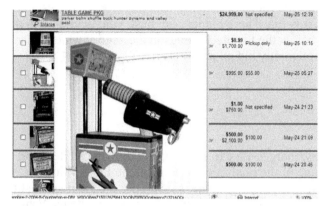

When the potential bidder hovers their mouse cursor over the Gallery Image, a larger image pops up.

Bold $1, Highlighting $5, Border $3

These options can highlight or bold the text of your auction. It can make your auction stand out in a crowded category. It is an inexpensive way of gaining more attention.

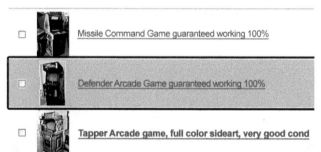

Top, normal listing.
Center, Highlighted listing.
Bottom, Bold listing

Value Pack

EBay offers varying combination offers for upgrades. Do the math and you may find the combo is worth the price for only a couple of upgrade features.

Those are the important options. Other options, like Gift Services, are not used except in special circumstances. Keep in mind, most members will find your listing by visiting the category or searching for specific keywords. Many of these upgrades are ways to make your auction stand out from other similar auctions. If you are selling a collectable and only a few others are listed, you may not need any of these upgrades except Gallery.

Hot Items

Why do sellers start bidding low? EBay has a feature called Hot Items. A hot item is any auction with more than 30 bids. By starting low, even at $0.99, you encourage the dream-bidders or thrill-bidder to place a bid. These are the people who bid a $5 then $6, then $7 on a $500 game console. They have no hope of actually winning at those prices, but they bid simply because they think it is fun. These bidders can push your auction into the Hot Zone. The Hot Zone is shown below the featured listings in a category which means many more people will see it and potentially bid on it.

Listing Fees

EBay does not charge bidders. EBay charges a fee to sellers when they list an item and when it sells they charge a percentage of the final sale price called the Final Value Fee. Listing fees range from $0.20 to $4.80 depending on the opening bid for the item. Listing Real Estate or Cars is more expensive, but these are much more expensive items. Vehicle listings are $40 or less and real estate listings are from $35 to $300 depending on the type of listing. There is no final value fee for Real Estate, only the listing fee.

Most of the small items being sold on eBay only incur a couple of dollars in listing fees even with the final value fee added. The seller should build this expense into the bid price. When deciding on your price, make sure you consider these fees

Basic fees

When you list an item on eBay, you're charged an Insertion Fee. If the item sells, you are also charged a Final Value Fee. The total cost of selling an item is the Insertion Fee plus the Final Value Fee.

Insertion Fees

Starting or Reserve Price	Insertion Fee
$0.01 - $0.99	$0.20
$1.00 - $9.99	$0.40
$10.00 - $24.99	$0.60
$25.00 - $49.99	$1.20
$50.00 - $199.99	$2.40
$200.00 - $499.99	$3.60
$500.00 or more	$4.80

Final Value Fees

Closing Price	Final Value Fee
Item not sold	No Fee
$0.01 - $25.00	5.25% of the closing value
$25.01 - $1,000.00	5.25% of the initial $25.00 ($1.31), **plus 3.25%** of the remaining closing value balance ($25.01 to $1,000.00)
Equal to or Over $1000.01	5.25% of the initial $25.00 ($1.31), **plus 3.25%** of the initial $25.01 - $1,000.00 ($31.69), **plus 1.50%** of the remaining closing value balance ($1000.01 - closing value)

EBay Fee Schedule from their website. These fees are subject to change so check the latest fees on the eBay website. Fees are also displayed before an auction is posted.

Typical listing fee scenario including closing Final Value Fee, and PayPal fees if this $0.99 item was paid by PayPal.	**Opening Bid $0.99** **Closing Bid $0.99** **Shipping $1.25** **Insertion Fee $0.20** **Final Value Fee $0.01** **Total EBay Fees $0.21** **PayPal Fee $0.34** **Total Fees $0.90** **Estimated Shipping $1.25** **Total Collected $2.24** **Profit $ 0.09**

Opening Bid $100 **Closing Bid $100** **Shipping $15** **Insertion Fee $2.40** **Final Value Fee $3.75** **Total EBay Fees $6.15** **PayPal Fee $3.64** **Total Fees $9.79** **Estimated Shipping $4.05** **Total Collected $115.00** **Net Profit $ 101.16**	**Typical listing fee scenario including closing Final Value Fee, and PayPal fees if this $100.00 item was paid by PayPal.**

This profit in the above examples do not consider the item's actual cost.

Offering a $100 item, that closes at $100, with $15 shipping costs a total in PayPal and eBay fees of $9.79. If you ship by Priority Mail at a cost of under $5 then the additional shipping and handling charges cover your listing and PayPal fees.

Some sellers list items over and over without thinking about the costs. You cannot continue listing an auction over and over and hope to make a profit. I saw a seller offer a Speedway arcade game for $365 over and over on eBay. Unfortunately this particular game, though fun to play, is very common and usually sells from $50 to $150 in non-working condition or $200-$300 in working condition. This seller's game was not working. He listed the auction more than ten times, each time paying $3.60 in insertion fees. He paid more than $36 in listing fees to relist the game. The game was worth less than $50 and he had already paid $36 trying to sell it. He was not watching his insertion fee and he did not know the value of the item. He did not learn from the first auction. When the game did not sell, he should have done more research or lowered the price. This seller kept running the same auction at the same high opening price and continued to receive no bids. He will be lucky to recover his money.

Most items sold are in the $20 to $50 range. If you offer an item at $30 and it closes at $30 with one bidder, and charge $8 shipping which is a pretty common auction, the total fees are $4.08 for eBay and PayPal. Again, the shipping and handling will cover the fees if this item can be shipped by Priority Mail flat rate.

	Opening Bid $30
	Closing Bid $30
	Shipping $8
Fees for a more common sale price of $30	Insertion Fee $1.20
on an eBay item. The total fees including	Final Value Fee $1.48
PayPal is only $4.08	Total EBay Fees $2.68
	PayPal Fee $1.40
	Total Fees $4.08
	Estimated Shipping $4.05
	Total Collected $38.00
	Net Profit $ 29.87

Note that these examples do not include any additional services such as Gallery or Buy-It-Now listing upgrades.

You can find eBay fee calculators at http://portal.dont-bid-on-it.com

I make sure my profit margin is high enough so I do not have to worry about a few dollars in eBay or PayPal fees. I avoid selling items that do not make enough to cover these fees.

Fees are not expensive, but you still need to keep track of your fees. There is an insertion fee which is charged every time you list an item whether it sells or not. If your item does not sell, you can relist the auction once by using the Relist, button and you will not be re-charged the insertion fee for the second auction, but only if it sells the second time. If the item does not sell the second time, you will be charged the fee. You cannot receive credit for upgrades like bold or highlight options.

OPENING BID

No Round Numbers! Your opening bid should not be a round number. EBay charges the initial listing fee based on your opening price. This fee is only pennies, but why pay more if you don't have to. You should list an item at 9.99, not 10.00. This will cost you less for the listing fee and it is a good price point. Using prices just below round numbers makes bidders feel like the item costs less than it really does. The 9.99 price point is used by retailers all the time. It works for auctions too.

Part IV Selling
Chapter 13 - Accepted Payments

Payment Methods

Make it clear what payment methods you accept. EBay has restrictions on what payment methods can be offered. This prevents criminals from setting up a fancy website claiming to offer payment services and then scamming innocent buyers. Beware of a seller who demands any unusual form of payment or insists on payment through a particular service other than PayPal. You can find a list of authorized payment methods in the Help Center of the eBay website.

> As of 2007 eBay allows these payment services
> **PayPal.com Allpay.net, Bidpay, cash2india, CertaPay,**
> **Checkfree.com, hyperwallet.com, Moneybookers.com,**
> **Nochex.com, Ozpay.biz, Paymate.com.au, Propay.com, XOOM**

Personal Checks

Payment by personal check is risky. Some people may have the money when they write the check, but not when you receive it. They may have forgotten about writing it and spend the money. You will be charged a returned check fee if the check does not clear. Now what do you do? Not only does the buyer owe you the original payment, but you are out the returned check fee too. Do you ask the buyer to cover the additional fee plus pay for the auction again with a good check? What if it also bounces?

When you receive a personal check you have to hold the item until the check clears which means you have to keep track of it. You have to know when the check clears and ship at that time. The buyer does not like this either because they have to wait for their items. It can take 7 to 10 days for a check to clear and it may be another week before your bank notifies you if it was returned. Personal checks are nothing but a headache. If you are running a serious eBay business, you can use an instant check service that automatically debits the persons account without having to process the check through a bank. This allows you to avoid returned check fees and you know if the check is good much faster. Checks are for paying the electric and gas bill, not for eBay purchases. Sending a check is risky for buyers too. Buyers are sending all of their banking information to someone they do not know. It is printed right on the check. Personal checks are not good for buyers or sellers.

Use your judgement on checks and money orders. If the buyer has a long history of positive transactions and there is nothing suspicious, you may want to ship early if the item is not expensive.

eChecks

Personal check problems can be avoided by using PayPal eChecks. A buyer can pay through PayPal and select the eCheck option. PayPal will debit their checking account and notify the seller when it clears. This is easy and much faster than waiting for a check to clear the bank. There are also never any bounced check fees when using PayPal's eChecks.

PayPal eChecks are the best option, but if your buyer does not want to use PayPal and insists on sending payment by mail, let the buyer know there will be a two week delay while the check or money order clears. Explaining the reason for the delay can often encourage the buyer to pay by PayPal.

Money Orders

Some people do not like to use PayPal or may not understand how PayPal works so they avoid it. Some people still do not have a credit card. These people will want to pay by another means and money order is the next best option. It is not perfect. Buyers may send fake money orders and they can send a money order and immediately file for a refund claiming it was stolen. You will not know this until after you shipped the goods. I have never had a money order returned to me, but I do not deal in high fraud items. If you send a money order outside of the USA, you need to purchase a special International money order otherwise it may not be honored. If an international buyer wants to send you a money order, they will need to send an international money order in US dollars. Expensive items should always be held until the money order clears the bank, just like checks.

Bidpay.com

BidPay allows bidders to use debit or credit cards to pay sellers. Bidpay.com is no longer a Western Union money order service. It is more like PayPal now.
There is no fee for buyers either. BidPay transfers money into the seller's bank account. Unlike PayPal, BidPay is strictly an auction payment service. A seller must have a BidPay account in order to accept payments. All of the security advice for PayPal and eBay apply to BidPay.

Western Union

Western Union money transfers can be sent to anyone. These are frequently used by criminals to request payments. Once sent, anyone in the country can claim the payment at any Western Union location. Western Union does have some security features and will require ID for large amounts, but it is not a perfect system. I never send payments by Western Union for auctions and distrust any seller who prefers or only accepts Western Union payments. Western Union even tells their customers on their own website not to use money transfer services to pay for online auctions. Western Union is great for sending emergency cash to someone you know, but be careful about sending money to anyone you do not know.

I will accept Western Union payments from buyers, but I do not list it as an option on my auctions. If a buyer wants to use this service I am happy to take it as a seller because it is irrevocable. Unfortunately it is irrevocable so the buyer has no protection if they send money to a dishonest seller.

CASH

Cash payments should never be requested in the auction. Any seller who asks for cash looks shady. The one exception is cash on pickup if the buyer picks up the item in person. Cash should not be sent by mail. If the letter is lost or delivered to the wrong address, the cash is lost. Now the buyer has sent payment and does not believe the seller when he says he never received the money. Avoid this problem and don't accept cash unless it is cash on pickup. EBay does not allow sellers to request cash by mail.

COD: CASH ON DELIVERY

It is hard to believe anyone uses COD anymore, but sometimes they request it. I never ship COD. Buyers are not home when the delivery company attempts delivery, the order comes back and now you are out the shipping costs for the first shipment plus the COD collection fee and you still have not been paid for the item. There is no security in shipping COD either. The buyer could just as easily receive a nicely packaged brick as the item ordered. The seller could receive a counterfeit cashier's check. COD requires extra paperwork and hassles. COD is not worth the trouble, use a better payment method.

CREDIT CARDS

If you are selling enough on eBay to justify your own credit card merchant account, then you should have your own website. If you have your own website then you may need a credit card merchant account. There is no need for a merchant account if you are a small seller. Buyers can still pay by credit card through PayPal. Buyers on eBay are not usually comfortable giving their credit card information to sellers. They will use PayPal to pay by credit card because they trust PayPal.

For a complete advanced techniques seller course, visit http://Bonus.DontBidOnit.com

PayPal

PayPal is by far the best payment method. It is fast, easy, and as secure as payments will ever be. The person sending you money does not even need a PayPal account. The buyer enters their credit card or bank account information in PayPal and you receive the payment to your PayPal account. You can transfer the money from your PayPal account to your bank account, receive it in the form of a check, or use it to pay for your own auction purchases. PayPal does charge the receiver of money a fee. This is simply the cost of doing business and it is not very much, thirty cents plus 2.9%. Not taking PayPal will not only cost you sales, it will make your overall bids lower because many potential bidders will not trust a seller who does not take PayPal.

I do not accept PayPal for high priced items. If someone buys something for more than $1000, then I require payment by cashier's check and I wait for it to clear. I even accept personal or business checks, but I wait for them to clear before shipping. When I do not accept PayPal for an auction, I always explain why. It is important for bidders to know why you have the payment terms you list.

"I accept only cash on pickup, or you can send cashier's checks, or personal/business checks(held until clear) for this item. Sorry, no PayPal on this item because it is worth over $1000"

> *I once sold an industrial DVD duplicator on eBay for $4000.00. I paid $7,000 for it a year earlier so the buyer got a great deal. It worked perfectly and it had just been refurbished from the factory. I offered a 30 day guarantee with it too. Ninety days after buying it and paying with PayPal, the buyer said the print cartridge (a $50 part) was not working and he wanted to return the entire $4000 machine for a refund. This sounded more than a little fishy and it was well past the warranty so I refused the return, but did offer to replace the $50 part even though it was well after my warranty period. He filed a reversal on his credit card and PayPal put a hold on the funds in my account. It took 6 months to complete the PayPal investigation, but they did side in my favor. This scammer tried to get the money back and keep the $4000 machine. After this experience I stopped taking large payments via PayPal.*
> *When you ship, make sure you have a tracking or delivery confirmation number. If there is a problem or a PayPal complaint, you will need it. I would have lost my $4000 if I could not have proven he received the duplicator.*

You cannot collect credit card information from a buyer directly and then enter it into PayPal. PayPal will track the IP and shut down your account or report you to law enforcement when they see one person entering several credit cards which are all credited to their own account. Only the buyer can complete the PayPal checkout process by entering their own information.

BUYER PREMIUM

Sellers cannot charge a premium for PayPal, credit cards, or any other payment method. PayPal takes a percentage of every transaction. Some sellers claim they will charge an extra fee above the auction price to cover PayPal fees, but they cannot charge more than the auction price. That would be against eBay rules. In California it is against the law to charge extra for credit card transactions. EBay is ruled by California law. You never have to pay a seller extra money for using a credit card or PayPal.

I avoid any seller who says the buyer must pay the PayPal fees. On a $100 item the fee is only about $3, and for a $20 item under $1. If the seller is selling something for $20 or $100 why is he nickel and diming the buyer for such a trivial amount? The seller should adjust the shipping charges or start the minimum bid higher. The buyer should not be penalized when paying immediately and using a method preferred by the seller. Buyers don't trust sellers who nickel and dime them. You can report sellers who attempt to charge Buyer Premiums to eBay.

INTERNATIONAL PAYMENTS

Checks, money orders, and credit cards are common in the USA. In other countries, they may not use checks. Money orders must be international money orders in US Dollars or they may be refused in the USA. Credit cards are not as common in other countries as they are in the USA.

PayPal is the best option for international payments. You avoid currency conversion problems, you avoid problems with payments being lost in the mail, and PayPal makes it easy for international buyers to open accounts. PayPal is the payment method of choice for international orders.

International bidders can be limited to paying via PayPal. You can specify in your auction that you only accept PayPal payments for international bidders. This is perfectly acceptable on eBay.

PAYMENT TERMS

Make it clear that you accept PayPal. Many bidders will pass over an auction that does not accept PayPal in favor of one that does. I am much less likely to bid on an auction from a seller who does not accept PayPal. I like to pay immediately by PayPal when I win an auction so the seller can ship my item quickly. I do not want to drive around town looking for a store that sells money orders, or wait in line at the post office for a money order, pay for the money order, then pay to mail a letter that will take days to arrive. Why does anyone bother paying this old fashioned way? The auction winner can click the Pay Now, button and pay by PayPal, immediately, and safely. I look for auctions that offer PayPal and avoid auctions that do not.

If you sell an item that must be picked up, then make sure you include in your terms pages a time limit. For example:

- Items not paid for within 7 days are subject to relisting and cancellation of the transaction.
- Items will be available for pickup for 30 days after the auction closes. Items not picked up within 30 days will be considered abandoned, the transaction cancelled, and the item may be resold. Any payments made will be considered a storage fee.

This gives you an option to resell the item if the buyer does not pick up. I have had buyers pay for items, then never show up to get them. I usually wait at least 60 days before reselling the item. Sometimes people buy items and forget. With PayPal it is easy to pay and forget you bought something because there is no credit card statement or reminder. Sometimes they buy items and realize they cannot use them but never think about the fact they already paid. I have also had people buy large items, pay half down, then 60 days later email with a hard-luck story and promise to pay the rest. How long can I hold a large item on the chance this person will pay. How long am I supposed to store HIS merchandise for free? I charge for storage of large items and small items. If someone pays and does not pick-up the item in a reasonable time the payment goes toward rent and the item is resold.

> *I purchased a decorative statue from someone in Australia for $12 plus $12 shipping. Only after the auction did I realize they didn't take PayPal. I had to send a money order. I sent a Western Union International money order because those are easy to cash in any country. When the seller received it, they said they could not find anywhere to cash it. This made no sense to me because it was a Western Union money order and any Western Union office could have cashed it, or their bank, or their post office(in Australia). The seller waited over two months after I sent payment to tell me they were having problems. I told them to forget about it. I had already given up after such a long time. They kept my money and never shipped what I paid for. If they had simply taken PayPal, they would have had the money and there would have been no problems. This is why you should take PayPal. PayPal is preferred by international buyers because many countries do not use checks and many people do not use credit cards in other countries. PayPal is a perfect option for them and there are no currency exchange rates to worry with. I will not buy from an international seller who does not accept PayPal.*

Beware of international money orders or cashier's checks. These are easy to counterfeit, and especially common for expensive items. Always wait for these to clear before shipping.

BANK TRANSFERS

You should never share your bank account information for a direct bank transfer. Direct transfers are common in Europe, but not in the USA. Criminals can drain your bank account if you share your information. If you conduct a lot of business in Europe, you can use your special secondary eBay bank account, discussed earlier, to accept transfers from European buyers if they request this option frequently.

Asking for your bank account number does not mean the buyer is planning to defraud you. Person to person bank transfers are common in Europe. It is simply a bad idea and not done in the USA between individuals. International buyers can always use PayPal which takes money from their bank account so PayPal is always the best option for international payments.

PAYMENT TYPES MEAN BUSINESS

The more payment options(within reason) you can offer, the more bidders will be attracted to your auctions. If you only accept PayPal then only those with PayPal accounts will bid which can reduce your overall closing price or sales. If you only accept Checks/Money Orders then people with PayPal accounts will pass over your auctions because of the inconvenience. It is best to accept PayPal and money orders for US orders.

Part IV Selling
Chapter 14 - Description

The description area is where most bidders make their buying decision. The description can sway an uncertain bidder towards the decision to bid or away from it. The description can make the difference between a high closing bid and a low closing bid or no bids at all.

Item Description

Make sure you include all of the important information about your item in the description. You should look at other auctions for similar items to see what information they list if you are unfamiliar with the item. You may find that your collectable is a special color that makes it more valuable or that everyone considers it important to know if the box is included. These details can make a difference in the final bid price. Make sure you include information potential bidders will need.

Repeat your title in the auction description. You should never list all of the information in the title and then leave the description sparse or empty.

Never assume that the buyer will 'just know' the size or weight of your item. People buy from eBay for many reasons and they may not be buying your item for the reason you expect.

The Description should answer these questions:

- Is there any damage(show in photos)
- Who made the item, the company, author, designer
- What is the model number if any
- What material is the item made from
- What is the size, color, weight. Include these even if you think they are unnecessary
- What is the item used for
- When was it made
- Is there a warranty
- Originality, has it been repainted, has it been repaired, is it in the original box, is it a first edition, or any information that applies to this specific category.
- What is the history of the item, when did you buy it, why are you selling it.
- Shipping and payment information

Think before posting your auction description. I have seen people selling language translator software for 14-languages but they do not list what the languages are. I have seen people selling vitamins but they do not say how many tablets are in the bottle. I have even seen big time power sellers selling books but they give no description about the book. All they give is a title with no information on what the book is about.

> *I recently needed a sprocket to repair an arcade game. All I knew was the size and the number of teeth. I searched auction after auction. There were many people selling lawn mower sprockets, but none of them bothered to list the size. Because of this, I bought the sprocket I needed from a website instead of an eBay seller. All of the eBay sellers assumed that the part number was enough. It was not. They should have listed the size of the sprocket and the number of teeth. Those eBay sellers lost a sale because they did not list enough information.*
>
> *I purchased a universal joint for a mechanical project and when I received it, I found out it was three inches long. I was expecting a large car part seven or eight inches in size. The seller did not specify the size and I bought based on the photo. I was not a happy buyer even though it was partly my fault for not asking the size before bidding. The seller should have included a size reference in the photograph and given dimensions.*

If you are selling a gear from an old lawnmower, don't assume someone is buying it for their lawnmower. They may want to use it in a metal sculpture and therefore need to know the dimensions. The buyer may have read somewhere that this gear will work with his garden tiller so he needs the size to compare before making a buying decision. If this information is not in your auction, the buyer will go to another auction and keep looking until someone gives him the information he needs. No matter what you are selling, give as much information as you can.

Potential bidders will rarely email to ask a question about the auction. Buyers will move on to another auction or assume your item is not the correct one if the important information is not listed. You have to anticipate the questions potential buyers will have then answer those questions in the description.

Weight is important. Even if you think no one cares about the weight, there will be a potential buyer wondering about the weight.

Never estimate the value of the item in the auction description. If you think your item is valuable and you say "*I have seen this item sell from $200 to $300 in the past*", you have limited the price you could receive. Potential bidders will assume the maximum value is $300 or less. They may think the seller is exaggerating the value which would make the value closer to $200. An inexperienced buyer may think the item is worth $500 until they read your description. Your estimate may also be wrong. This item may be a special color or a special version that is extremely rare and more valuable. Quoting a low estimate may cause bidders to assume your item is not the rare and expensive version. Quoting a high estimate will make experienced bidders, who know the value, mistrust the seller. The only true value of the item is what it sells for. Never give an estimate of value.

If you sell clothing, make sure you list the size and any damage. If you sell car parts, make sure you list the vehicle the part is for.

Catch Buyers Interest

Make your listing interesting. You do not need any fancy graphics. Just tell the story of your item. If you found it in the attic, say so. If you won it in a contest, let people know. But, don't say you bought it at a yard sale last week for $10 and hope to sell it for $100. It is better not to say anything than to say you bought it cheap. Buyers will think it is a cheap item or something is wrong with it. Do not say anything if you purchased the item to resell on eBay. Your story should be interesting, but you do not have to say everything. Explain how the item can be used. Let readers know who you think would be most interested in the item and why. Say positive things about the item and tell a story that will capture a buyer's interest.

Knowing the item's history can make people feel closer to the item and they are more likely to bid on it. They will bid higher than they would if you only listed the basic information. This is how to encourage emotional bidding. Emotional bidders will often bid more than the item is worth. A good story can add value to your item beyond nickels and dimes. A good story can make emotional bidders want it more.

If you have an old family photo showing the item, include a printed copy of the photo on glossy paper as part of the auction. If you have the original receipt from the 1920's, include that. Little things like these can add a great deal of perceived value to an otherwise common item.

Tell the whole truth, but start with the positives. If the item is scratched, you have to tell potential buyers, but you can always start by describing the positive aspects.

This antique lamp is in great condition. It has never been repainted. I used it for years on my desk, but it no longer fits my new décor. It would be a perfect addition to any office or lamp collection. There is a two inch scratch along the top as shown in the photo. If you have any questions feel free to contact me. I hope you will enjoy this lamp as much as I have in the past years. Good luck bidding.

It is always nice to wish potential bidders good luck. This sends a message of *'Now you know the facts; go and place your bid so you can win, I'm behind you all the way'*. Simply saying Good Luck can double the number of bids on some auctions.

Keep it Positive

Remember to make your auction listing positive.
> **Do say "I gladly accept PayPal and money orders"**
> **Don't say "PayPal only, I don't take personal checks"**
> **Don't say "No checks, Don't Ask"**

Keep your wording positive and avoid using No or Never.

NOTHING FANCY

Don't use sounds, fancy html, or java scripts.

Some inexperienced sellers insert java scripts that change the viewer's cursor, cause funny characters to appear, or any host of other annoying actions. The majority of auction visitors will be offended by these types of scripts. In order to run these scripts, you must run a program on the auction viewer's computer. You should not run code on someone else's computer without their permission. These gimmicks may seem cute to inexperienced computer users, but the majority of bidders will find them annoying. When I open an auction and a character pops up or my cursor changes to a silly streaming banner, I click the back button immediately and look for another auction.

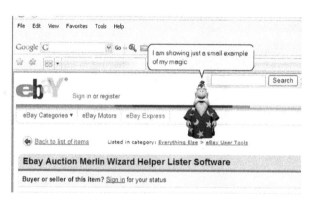

Pop Up characters may seem cute, but they drive away bidders. Most computer users dislike other people running scripts on their computer and will immediately click the Back Button when a character pops up, music starts playing, a computer generated voice automatically starts or the cursor changes into a streaming banner or other animation. You never know what else this script may be doing in the background.

These scripts distract users from the auction. Viewers may be more interested in playing with your java script than in reading the description. Keep it simple and never run code on other people's computers without their permission.

Auctions are not the place to show off your web design prowess. They should be simple, show the information needed, and that is all. Putting a lot of web images, fancy tables or designs, only confuses potential bidders.

Don't use animated gifs. These are distracting and will make your auction look cheap. You want the potential bidder to place a bid, not be distracted and lose focus from the item you are auctioning.

When bidders click on an auction and hear an audio file, music, or those annoying computer generated voices, they usually click the back button and look for another auction. Music may sound good on your computer, but on another person's computer it may be choppy if their Internet connection is slow, it may slow their computer down, and it can delay the loading of photos making the viewer think there are no photos. If you are going to use music or sound files, do not set them to auto-play. Give the viewer a play button. Visitors can listen when/if they want. Don't auto play. That is annoying and it will cost you bids.

Some bidders surf eBay from work or in the family room late at night when the kids are asleep. They do not expect sounds to play and if they click an auction that auto plays music or a voice, they will immediately click the back button, curse at the seller and never return.

EBay offers a Listing Designer which will add fancy borders and fonts to your auction. These only distract viewers and should not be used. Stick to the basics and keep the auction clean and clear.

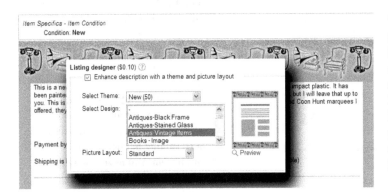

The Listing Designer adds a fancy border to auction descriptions for an additional fee. Excess graphics or HTML can distract potential bidders or make the auction look busy.

ABBREVIATIONS

If you use abbreviations, include the translation. Not all buyers may recognize your abbreviation and even if they should recognize it, their brain may not be working 100% at 2 A.M. when they see the auction. If you describe an item as NIB show it as NIB(New In Box). Even experienced eBay buyers may not recognize an abbreviation. Is NRMT Near Mint or No Reserve, Mint Condition? Does COA mean Certificate of Authenticity, California Orthopaedic Association, Change of Address, Canadian Osteopathic Association, or Coat of Arms? It means all of them. The same acronyms and abbreviations mean different things in different fields.

If you confuse buyers or talk above their head, they will not be comfortable bidding on your auction. When you use an acronym or abbreviation, also explain what it means.

DON'T THREATEN BUYERS

It is never appropriate to threaten potential buyers with negative feedback or reports to law enforcement if they do not pay.

Hot headed sellers sometimes state in their auctions

> **"I require payment in 3 days and I will report anyone who has not paid by then to eBay as a non paying bidder."**

I am only looking at this person's auction and I already do not like him. I am certainly not going to bid on his auction because he is clearly unreasonable. Three days is much too short of a time to expect payment. What if the buyer used a snipe bidding program and won on Friday of a three day weekend. He might not know he won until he checked his email Tuesday. If the buyer has to purchase and mail a money order or transfer money to his PayPal account, it will take more than three days too. If a bidder uses Buy-It-Now on Friday will the seller leave negative feedback on Monday if the seller has not received their check? Three days is unreasonable. Seven to ten days is more reasonable, but even then you should not state it in the auction. The buyer knows he must pay. Giving a schedule makes a buyer feel trapped even if they would pay immediately on their own. Using schedules only gives buyers a reason not to bid. Never demand payment on a schedule. Do not put too many restrictions in the auction.

Never say *"Don't bid if you don't intend to pay"* This will never deter a non paying bidder and it puts off honest bidders because it makes the seller seem difficult and angry.

Statements like these drive away buyers. Don't threaten potential bidders.

MEASUREMENTS

When including measurements in a description make sure you remember that eBay is a world-wide website. I see a lot of sellers outside the US making a common mistake in measurements. They include metric only measurements in their auctions. These numbers mean nothing to Americans and the USA is the biggest buyer on eBay. Every auction that needs any measurement should be in standard Imperial units and also in metric units so it is clear and easy to understand for everyone. When I see an auction offering 420 cm of wire, I look for another auction. I am too lazy to do the math and figure out if this is the length in inches I need and the same is true of most people who are shopping for something of a specific size or weight. They simply will not bother to do the conversion.

POSTING YOUR PHONE NUMBER

You may want to give a phone number for people to call with questions, but you also do not want to give out your home or personal number. You can rent a toll free number. Toll free numbers cost a few dollars a month and you can forward them to your home phone. You can set them to only ring during certain times of the day and to go to voice mail at other times so you do not receive calls at midnight asking about an auction. EBay is an international website as well as national. If you post your phone number, someone in Europe may call at midnight without thinking about the time difference.

There are many companies offering toll free services on the Internet. Some of these offer extremely poor service and some are downright dishonest. Do some research before signing up with any toll free service. Check out the services they offer too. You can check out kall8.com for basic toll free number service. They are inexpensive and reliable. You can find other toll free services on our recommended page at http://portal.dont-bid-on-it.com

I would never advise anyone to list personal home number in an auction. Use a toll free service or a VOIP service. You can signup for VOIP(voice over IP) services which provide Internet based telephone service. This gives you an alternate phone number that works through your high speed Internet service.

Phone numbers are only important on expensive items where the buyer may be wary about doing business for such a large amount of money. On small items, it is not important and it would be abnormal for someone to call and ask questions about a $20 or $30 item instead of emailing.

KEEP IT BRIEF

You want your description to be complete, but brief.

Don't go on and on with your description. If it is ten paragraphs long, no one will want to read it. Stick to the subject of the auction as well. Don't go into your business history, your family history, or your life story. Long and pointless auction listings make people lose interest. Put all of the important information in the first paragraph. If you need more information, you can include other paragraphs with titles like Detailed Specifications or Item History. You can link to the manufacturer's website if they have a page listing things like electrical specifications that a user may want to know.

> *When a potential bidder is looking at your auction you want to answer the unspoken question "Why should I buy from you instead of another seller?" The description can answer this by stating your guarantee or emphasizing low shipping costs.*

SOAP BOX AUCTIONS

It is never appropriate to use an auction listing as a forum for a political idea or to bash a company you do not like. Buyers do not care about your religious or political beliefs and are turned off by sellers who use auctions as soap box forums even if the message is a positive one, even if it is a message they agree with. If you went into a store and the clerk began telling you why you should share his political beliefs would you come back to that store again? Not likely. It is simply not appropriate to use an auction as a soap-box forum. Auctions are a form of business communications. Business etiquette applies.

Posting complaints makes potential buyers wonder if the seller is a reasonable person. Once they begin wondering, they start looking for reasons to not bid. Keep such postings in your personal blog, not in an auction.

Auction listings are not the place to complain about eBay services or PayPal. These are large companies that service hundreds of millions of people yearly. There will always be some people who are dissatisfied about something, some people who were caught with their hand in the cookie jar, some people who simply enjoy complaining about corporations. An auction is not the place for these complaints. If a potential bidder sees an auction where the seller goes on and on complaining about how PayPal ripped him off, but the potential buyer has never had a problem with PayPal, the buyer will question the integrity of the seller and rightfully so. If there is a problem with the transaction, is this how the seller will treat the potential buyer? Such rants drive away potential bidders. Most of the complaints could have been avoided if the seller had followed the recommendations in this program.

The one person who takes offense with your statement may have been the one who would have been your highest bidder. Soap box statements will drive away bidders. Anti company statements make the seller seem angry and difficult. Don't give potential bidders a reason to not bid.

FEEDBACK CHALLENGE

Never state in your auction "**I have a 100% positive feedback rating, you can trust me**". If your feedback is perfect, that is great and people will notice. Stating it in your auction can attract undesirable bidders who are thinking "*100%? we will see about that*". Before you know it, you have a problem bidder buying something with the intention of leaving negative feedback just because he can. Don't invite trouble. Smart bidders will always check your feedback on their own.

List your return policy in every auction. A clear return policy makes buyers feel more confident in you and what you are selling. Ten to thirty days is plenty of time for the buyer to decide if the item is what was advertised. There is no point in offering a return policy with a long list of exclusions. The longer the list of exclusions, the more the buyer will think the seller is trying to back out of their returns policy before making the sale. Keep your return policy simple. If your products are accurately described you should have very few returns.

100% satisfaction guarantee, except product must be returned in original box within 2 days, postage paid, with a 20% restocking fee charge, must obtain rma number by calling our number between 8am to 9am Guam time and item must be returned within 24 hours of receiving rma, Jupiter must be in Sagittarius or no refunds will be accepted for the month.

Example of a poor return policy

My policy is a 10 day satisfaction guarantee. If someone receives an item they do not like, they can return it for a refund minus shipping. This should take care of any unhappy customers and make negative feedback unnecessary. Unfortunately there are people who want to leave negative feedback for the thrill of bad-mouthing a seller. This is why I append to my policy on my AboutMe page a statement which says the return policy is voided if the buyer leaves negative feedback anywhere or files for a refund or chargeback without giving me adequate opportunity to resolve the matter. Negative feedback negates any claim the buyer has for support or return privileges. I do not state this in the auction, but it is on the About Me page under terms. In the auction I state that I have a 10 day, or 30 day for some items, satisfaction guarantee and then link to the About Me page for details.

A risk of a 'not as advertised' policy is that buyers will buy from you with the intention of committing fraud or you may attract buyers who are addicted to buying. They will buy the item, then when they receive it, they damage it and send you a picture claiming it was not as advertised so they can receive a refund. A satisfaction guarantee policy is much better. If the buyer is not satisfied they can return the item for a refund. If a buyer does return an item and it really was damaged, even if it is the fault of the postal service, I will give a full refund including shipping even though my policy says I do not have to. This makes for a happy customer that may buy more items.

Never sell items **as-is**. This does not build buyer confidence. Even if you are offering a broken radio for parts, give a guarantee that it is as-listed. Your listing should state the radio is broken, clearly say why it is not working, describe any damage, and then guarantee that the item is as listed or it can be returned for a refund. Any reasonable buyer will buy it for parts and will not return it. Giving that extra bit of confidence with a return option can generate a sale or a higher bid than you might have received without it.

A counter is a small display at the bottom of the auction showing how many people have viewed the auction. They can be useful to determine how effective the title and gallery image are. They can show how popular the listing is. If the seller has very few people viewing the listing, then either the title keywords are bad or the gallery image is not attracting viewers. If there are a lot of views, but no bids, this may mean the description is missing something or there is another problem with the listing.

A counter is especially good if you expect snipe bids. Remember that your serious bidders will not bid until the last minute. It can be hard to gauge interest when bidders wait until the last minute to bid. You may want to use some type of counter to see how many people are looking at your auction.

You should never us a visible counter when you create an auction. This type of counter shows everyone how many people have seen your auction. If the number is low, bidders may think there is no interest so your item must be uninteresting and will not bid. If the number is high and there are few bids, potential bidders will think others have already reviewed your auction and decided it was not worth bidding on. Don't give potential bidders a reason not to bid.

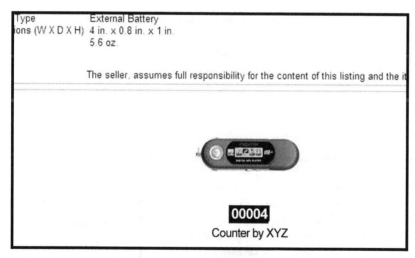

Visible counters should not be used in auctions. Use hidden counters or no counter instead.

You can select an option to use a counter that is only visible to the seller. If you use a counter, make sure you select this option.

I never use counters in my auctions. If everything is setup correctly, they are not needed unless you are doing your own market research. You can track views and watchers under your MyEbay page for items you are selling.

PART IV SELLING
CHAPTER 15 - PHOTOS

You should never list an auction without posting a photo. A good photo can stimulate buying interest in someone who was only browsing. People shop visually.

A good photo can make the difference between a sale and no sale, between a high closing bid and a low closing bid. Good photos can attract high bidders and bad photos will drive them away. Taking the best possible photos can make or break your auction.

Many auctions have received no bids because bidders had no idea what the seller was actually selling. Their photos were so bad you could not see the item.

Auctions without photos look shady. Potential buyers cannot see what they are buying and it makes them question whether or not the seller actually has the item. Photos are important on both inexpensive and expensive items. Photos are important even if you think everyone knows what the item looks like.

You should take full shots and close-ups. If your item has any damage, any model numbers, or any other information the buyer might be interested in, take close-up photos of it. Photos should be clear and well illuminated. The background should not be filled with clutter.

The easiest way to add photos to your auction is to upload your photos to eBay using their photo hosting service. All you have to do is select the photos on your computer and they will be uploaded and displayed in the auction. If you have your own web space or your own domain, you can add links to your photos in the auction. This saves you from paying for additional photos(which eBay charges to show). There are third party hosting companies that will host your photos so they can be seen on eBay. They generally post ads for their company in your listing under the photos. EBay's photo service works pretty well, allows for large pictures and is the easiest way to go. I always use eBay's photo service or my own hosting.

You do not have to be a professional photographer to take a good photo of your item. Digital cameras make taking photos easy and inexpensive. Digital is much better than film. You will know immediately if the photo needs to be retaken. It costs nothing to take more photos when using a digital camera. With digital cameras, you never have to pay for processing or wait for them photos to be developed. If you do not have a digital camera, you can buy a new or used one on eBay. You do not need a fancy or expensive camera. A good one megapixel or higher camera will do a great job. A higher megapixel camera is great for vacations, but on eBay you do not need giant images.

Many digital cameras are sold with only enough memory to take one high quality photo. Camera companies do this to make buyers purchase additional memory cards. You may not need to purchase additional memory because you will only take a few item photos at a time. If you do need more memory, get an inexpensive card. You can take a few photos and then transfer them to your computer.

You may have an instant camera or a traditional film camera you really like. Don't use it. It simply is not worth the trouble and cost. Digital cameras can be purchased for less than you would spend on a few rolls of film plus developing costs. Not to mention the wasted time waiting for the photos to be developed, carrying them to the developer, picking them up. Instant cameras do not have the quality or features needed for eBay item photos.

There are many considerations when buying a digital camera if you are using it for vacation photos. For that kind of camera you need to consider things like memory, zoom, image stabilization, image quality and other features. Your eBay camera does not require as much thought.

If you already have a digital camera then you can use it. If you are buying one for eBay photos, go for an inexpensive camera. Not necessarily the cheapest one out there, but not an expensive one either. You do not need all of the fancy features you would for a camera you take on vacation and you don't care if it has some scratches on the case. Zoom does not matter. You never need to change lenses. You can move the camera closer and farther from your item so you never use zoom or a different lens. Image stabilization is not important because you will be able to use both hands to steady the camera. A basic camera will do the job.

Inexpensive digital cameras take excellent photos and are the perfect choice for eBay auction images.

There are some features you will want in your digital eBay camera. You do want an LCD display screen on the back so you can see what your photo will look like. You want a camera with a Macro mode. Almost any modern camera will have these features and more. It is hard to go wrong unless you buy a child's toy camera.

eBay Cameras should have
LCD Display
Macro Mode

The default image format for most cameras is jpg, pronounced J-peg. This is the best format to use for eBay photos.

Most digital cameras include an LCD display that lets you see exactly what your photo will look like.

Macro Mode is usually selected using a flower icon. This indicates close-up photo taking mode and will take crisp in-focus shots very close to the item.

Set your camera to 800x600 or as close as your settings allow. Your camera manual will tell you which quality setting to use and how to set your camera for that size. Larger images are good, but there is no reason to take gigantic images. Sizes above 1024x768 are unnecessary. EBay will automatically downsize your image to the correct size so it looks good on screen if you use their hosting service.

If you host your own images on your website instead of the eBay picture viewer, be careful not to make the pictures too large. If your images are too large you can lose bidders. Large photos that run off the screen are a sign of an inexperienced seller. If the large image takes too long to load, potential bidders may think there is no image and click the back button before the image appears. Using the eBay picture viewer avoids this problem.

DON'T STEAL

You should never copy photos from another auction. That is stealing. Take your own photos.

When someone takes a photograph, they automatically own the copyright to that photo. It is a violation of copyright laws to use someone's photo without their permission. It is also a violation of eBay policy. Your account can be suspended if you copy images from someone else's auction. Copying images from manufacturer's websites is quite common, but it is also a violation of copyright law. It is unlikely a large company will complain because you used an image of their xyz laptop in your auction to sell your old xyz laptop, but it is still a violation of copyright law. There are some companies that watch eBay auctions and do file a VeRO(eBay's Verified Rights Owner program) complaint when someone uses their photos without permission.

Buyers also trust a seller with real photos more than one who copies images from a manufacturer's website. Many bidders monitor eBay categories closely. If they see photos in your auction and remember they were in another auction, they will not trust you. They may not believe you even have the item if the photos were copied from another auction. You should always take your own photographs of the actual item being sold. Buyers can easily tell when you are using a photo from the manufacturer's website. Buyers want to see the actual item they are bidding on, not a stock image. Using an actual photo you took can increase the number and amount of bids.

Never take a photo of your item surrounded by other items. The image is cluttered and it is not always clear what is being sold.

How to Take Photos

Most items sold on eBay are smaller items. They can be easily photographed in a chair. I like to use a chair because it has a back and arms which make a good background when covered. Chairs are easy to move into the best light or even outdoors.

Make your item stand out against the background. Use dark colored backgrounds for light colored items and white for dark colored items.

Placing a bed sheet or solid color towels over the chair can create an excellent contrasting background. The background does not have to be perfectly smooth. Wrinkles add texture to the image. You can use solid color poster board or you may have a chair that is already upholstered in solid black or white.

A chair makes a good platform to take photos of smaller items. You can use a table or the floor as long as the background is a solid light or dark color.

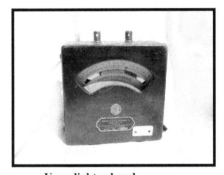

Use a light colored background for dark colored items and a dark colored background for light colored items.

Take photos of the front, back, and close-ups of any important parts, any damaged areas, part numbers, or labels.

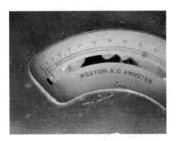

Most digital cameras have a Macro setting. This is the close up picture taking setting. It is important to select this setting when taking photos a few inches from the item. The Macro Setting will keep your close up photos in focus and adjust the light balance correctly. If you do not use the Macro setting, extreme close-ups may be blurry.

Use the standard automatic setting if you are taking a photo of a large item like a computer.

Larger items should be photographed against a plain background. You can hang bed sheets behind larger items or simply move them in front of solid color walls.

Photo Checklist
- *Photograph dark items on light background*
- *Photograph light items on dark background*
- *No clutter around the item*
- *Clear close-ups using Macro setting*
- *Don't use other people's photos*

Sometimes you need a visual reference in your photograph. Giving the size is not always enough. If an item is small you should have a visual reference that shows its relative size. This might be a quarter in the shot or a CD or a pencil. Giving the dimensions in the description is not enough for some items. The bidder needs to *understand* the size and this requires a visual reference.

Use a visual reference like a quarter, pencil, or CD to indicate the size of your item. This is especially important on small items.

Don't assume your potential buyer will just know the size. They may know more about the item than you do. Buyers may be looking for a rare larger or smaller version of the item if it is a collectable.

Take photos of all angles. Top, bottom, right, left, everything. Many buyers have told me about receiving an item and finding out the one side that was not shown in the auction was the one with damage. Take photos of everything, even of the blank bottoms or backs of clocks. If you are selling a shirt, take a photo of the front and the back. This will only build buyer's confidence in you and the item being sold.

If your item has any damage, any model numbers, or any other information the buyer might be interested in, get close-up photos of it.

If your item is in the original box, make sure to scan or take photos of the box. When it comes to collectables, the box may be worth more than the item that came in it.

You do not need any fancy lighting. Your item should be well lit and try not to use the flash. Flash causes reflections and can make an item look flat and less appealing. It can cause hot spots on items with shiny finishes or glass. Turn on lights around the item so your camera's auto flash feature does not want to flash. Make sure your lights are not colored. If they shine through a lamp shade, your item may look yellow. You can take the shade off for your eBay photos.

If possible, take your photos outside where you have plenty of sunlight. Your camera should adjust the lighting automatically and no flash is needed.

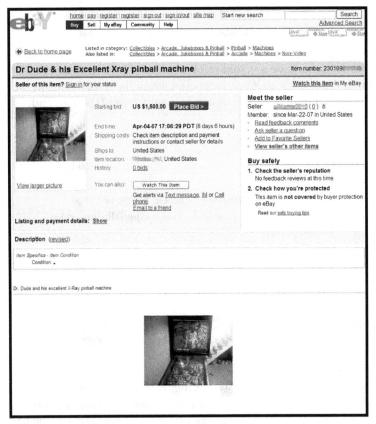

Example of a terrible auction. Seller has a new account with a zero feedback rating. They are attempting to sell a $1,500 pinball game. They give no information, no close-ups and the only image is so blurry, you cannot see what the game looks like. They do not say whether or not it works, but they expect someone to bid $1,500 or more for it. This game is only worth $200-$300 in working condition based on similar auctions. Do you trust this seller? Would you bid on this auction?

The pinball groups are actually excellent places to find examples of proper auctions. Pinball people often take great care in their listings and provide plenty of information and lots of close up photos. Check the Pinball groups for good examples of how to post an auction.

Jewelry, or any reflective item, can be difficult to photograph. To properly photograph reflective items surround them with diffuse light. That may sound like a complicated photographer's word, but it is really simple. Direct light from a light bulb or a camera's flash causes reflections. Diffused light is very even. You can reflect light off of white walls or white posterboard, or use white cloth to diffuse the light from a bulb. This will make the light evenly cover the item which avoids hot-spots and reflections.

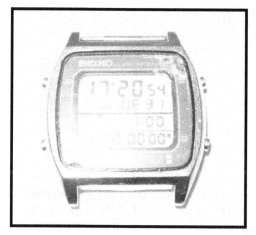

Camera flash or direct light from light bulbs can cause reflections which make the item look bad.

Using diffused light without flash makes the item clear. This item looks much clearer and will attract more bids.

If you take lots of photos of shiny items, you may want to make a special diffusion box. Professional photographers use similar boxes for photographing jewelry. Instead of placing your item on a cloth and taking a photo, place it in a box that is painted white inside. Shine your light in from one side through a white cloth or paper. This will make an even light that bounces all around the inside of the box. Cut a hole in the top or side of the box that is large enough for your camera. Take a photo by aiming through the hole. The reflective item is surrounded by light so there are no harsh reflections.

If you sell one item over and over, like a wristwatch if you have a case of 100 wristwatches, take multiple angles on it and post several auctions as if they are all different auctions by different people. They all have different photos and descriptions. Take one on photo the carpet, one with a professional looking all white background, then another with a black background, one with lots of angles, another set of shots with only three angles, another face on, then a 3/4 angle, etc. Post each to an auction and make each auction look a little different. If someone is not attracted to one photo, they may be to another. Then see which has the most sales, which the least. Replace the poorest seller with another set of photos and keep changing until you have a set of auctions that are hot sellers. You will find one or some auctions have much higher sales than others.

POSTCARDS, STAMPS, OR PAPER ITEMS

There is no need to take a photo if you are selling a postcard or flat paper item. Simply lay the item on your scanner and scan it. Re-size with software to the desired size. You can lay a quarter on the scanner to act as a size reference. Using a scanner is the best option when selling small items like stamps or coins. It allows you to capture details that would be very difficult to see with a photograph. Inexpensive scanners for $20 and $30 do an excellent job.

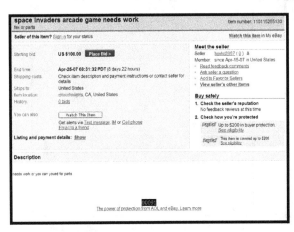

Example of a terrible auction. The seller has a new account with a zero feedback rating. They are attempting to sell an arcade video game, but there is no photo and no information. In the description they say "*needs work or you can youed for parts*". Apparently the seller was unable to proofread their one sentence fragment. There is no information about what parts are included, why the game does not work, no terms, nothing. No one could bid on this auction because they have no idea what they are actually bidding on. The grammar is also a tip-off that this would be a problem seller.

> *Pressing the snap-picture button can sometimes cause the camera to move which results in a blurry photo. Avoid blur in low light by using the timer. When you use the built in timer, you do not have to press the button and can hold the camera steady. You can also brace your arm against a solid surface, place the camera on a table, or use a tripod for steady shots.*

PHOTO DON'TS

Make sure you do not take a photo of one collectible among other collectables. You will receive messages from eBay members asking about the other items in the photo and if they are available for sale.

> *I once saw an arcade game on eBay and the seller had it surrounded by several other antique games. I emailed to ask if the others were for sale and he said they were, but he had not listed them yet. I made an offer and he accepted. Was it a sleazy backdoor deal? No, because they had not yet been listed. I picked up a number of collectable games before anyone else.*

Don't post photos sideways. Post them in the correct orientation so bidders do not have to figure out what you are selling, or turn their head to see it. Sideways photos are unprofessional.

Don't think your item does not need a photo. Always post a photo. If you are selling a computer video card and you think everyone knows what it looks like, post a photo anyway. If you are selling a laptop and fifty other people have the same model listed, show a photo of your actual laptop anyway. It lets the bidder know that you actually have the item you are offering.

Never assume that the buyer is familiar with what you are selling. They may be trying to find a specific computer video card with a specific revision and chips in certain locations. Maybe your computer video card photo shows this specific feature the bidder is looking for. With no photo they would pass over your auction.

> *I once needed a video card with a TV-Out port. I knew the card brand and model I needed, but there were different versions with different ports. I went through twenty auctions where none of the sellers listed the ports on the card or showed a photo other than a blurry stock image from the manufacturer's website. I finally found someone who posted a photo of the actual card being sold and it had the port I needed. That is the seller who made a sale out of twenty-one sellers. Never underestimate the power of a good photo.*

IMAGE SOFTWARE

If you are familiar with image editing tools or comfortable using a computer, you can use editing software to change your photo. Many cameras come with image editing software. You can also download free software from the Internet. Software will allow you to adjust the brightness and crop an image to remove any unwanted background items.

The programs Picasa for PC and Mac or IPhoto for Mac are free and can be used to edit photos. Picasa is from Google and available at http://picasa.google.com/
IPhoto should already be installed on your Mac.

GALLERY IMAGE

Plan ahead for your gallery image. This is the small image that appears next to your listing in search results. You want to take a photo that will be clear when it is small so viewers will immediately know what the item is. Choosing a solid color background that hilights your item will make it stand out. You can select which image is the Gallery Image if you are posting more than one.

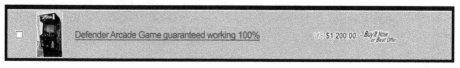

PART IV SELLING
CHAPTER 16 - DEALING WITH BUYERS

BUYER QUESTIONS

During the auction you may receive questions from interested buyers. Communications with buyers should always be done through the eBay Message Center. Using the eBay Message Center keeps a record of all correspondence. Some people have unreliable email services which may mean lost email. Even if their email is lost they can still read your message on eBay.

Responding to these questions using the eBay Message Center provides proof that you have communicated with customers and that you have attempted to resolve any problems they claim to have had. This on-eBay record is important if there is a problem later.

You may receive questions that should not be responded to. Some people ask pointless questions, such as 'what is it' type questions. These people are called trolls. They troll the Internet asking pointless questions. They are not serious buyers, they simply like to go around asking questions to see if anyone will respond. If you post an auction offering an external computer harddrive and you receive a question asking "What is this for" you can ignore it. Why would someone be interested in bidding on your auction if they have no idea what they would be bidding on? The person who asks this type of question is not an actual buyer they are trolls. Ignore trolls.

Another pointless question is the 'How dare you...' type. This may be a *how dare you charge $10 when I can buy the same thing locally for $5* email or *how dare you charge $2 shipping when it will fit in a first class envelope* email. Of course, the person does not consider the differences in your product or the fact that you ship the item to someone's door. These people are also not serious buyers and they only email for the thrill of complaining. They should be ignored. By the next day, they will have forgotten about the email and they may have sent ten others to other sellers. If you respond, they will be reminded of their email and they will have the thrill of trying to start an argument to prove they are right. Ignore these people. If they are not potential buyers, they are wasting your time.

If you receive a how-dare-you message or any other inciting message, add the person to your blocked bidder list right away. These are problem customers looking to pick a fight or cause problems.

Never tell a buyer to read the description. Even when the description is clear, someone can miss the shipping costs at the bottom or a size or weight. You may find your polite response was to the high bidder at the end of the auction.

People find it easy to be rude when they are not communicating face to face. Keep this in mind both when reading and sending messages. If you receive a rude or angry message, a polite response can quickly bring the person back into the polite zone and they may even apologize for their previous email. An angry response will guarantee they are not only going to respond in an angry fashion, but they will not be bidding on your auctions. If a polite email is all it takes to sell an item for $100 instead of $50, it is easily worth it.

If you are rude to a customer you should immediately send an apology. The customer may read the rude email first and respond to it before reading the apology, but that is OK. You will receive their angry reply first, but watch for their response to the apology if they send one. You at least have the apology out there and it may repair some of the damage a rude email made.

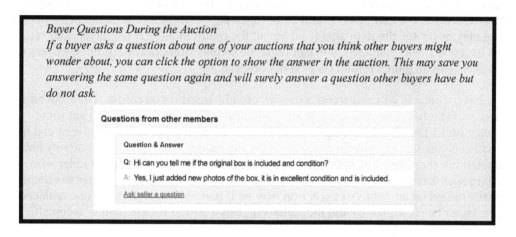

Buyer Questions During the Auction
If a buyer asks a question about one of your auctions that you think other buyers might wonder about, you can click the option to show the answer in the auction. This may save you answering the same question again and will surely answer a question other buyers have but do not ask.

Questions from other members

Question & Answer

Q: Hi can you tell me if the original box is included and condition?

A: Yes, I just added new photos of the box, it is in excellent condition and is included.

Ask seller a question

EBAY MESSAGE CENTER

If a buyer complains, it will always be in your interest to communicate using the eBay message center and to be polite. Start off your response with a disarming statement that will let the buyer know you understand their concern.

I am sorry you were not satisfied with the item's color. How would you like to resolve the problem? I can offer a full refund for the returned item if you would like to return it plus I will pay for the return shipping or I can offer $5 back and you keep the item if that will make up for the color difference.

Many times the buyer will decide to keep the item anyway. Keep your responses short and to the point. Don't belittle the buyer by reminding him you have a thousand positive feedbacks and he has ten. Don't threaten the buyer with negative feedback. If the buyer threatens to give you negative feedback, you can remind them it is your policy to give like feedback for feedback received.

Some items I sell are purchased in large lots for very little money per piece. If the item is not expensive to replace or not worth shipping back, and the buyer says they will return the item. I may send the refund or replacement and tell the customer not to bother returning the item. You might still get positive feedback out of this bad transaction. Most buyers are honest and will not try to obtain a fraudulent refund. There is no reason to pay return shipping on a broken item you cannot resell or to pay $5 to return an item you purchased in a lot for fifty cents each.

This may seem like a loss, but if your products are good and accurately described, you should have very few returns or dissatisfied customers. It is worth losing a few dollars on one sale to keep your feedback and you may make up the money on a sale to the same customer later.

A buyer may receive an expensive item and demand a refund, but they do not want to return the item. I require a return in these cases. I will even pay for return shipping once I have received the item. Don't send an advance payment for a returned item's shipping. You may never see the item again and be out the return money. If the buyer does return the item and it was damaged, you can issue the refund. Sometimes dishonest buyers will use this tactic to gain a refund they do not deserve.

If a buyer contacts you and wants a partial refund I suggest you refuse. They can return the item for a full refund or none at all. Dishonest buyers try this tactic to get some money back. They have nothing to lose. They make up a problem or complaint and then email every seller they buy from asking for some money back. If they get money back great, if not they have lost nothing. This is an unethical tactic. I add any bidder who makes such a request to my blocked bidder list. It is unusual for a customer to accept a partial refund on an item. An exception may be if part is broken that must be replaced. If a customer has complained and the seller suggests a partial refund, that is acceptable.

You do not have to deal with customers who are intentionally rude. You should try to diffuse the situation and satisfy a reasonable customer. Try to look at the situation from their point of view. Some customers simply want their concerns heard and are not looking for a return or refund. If they are unreasonable or continue to be explicitly rude, you do not have to deal with them. There is no reason to waste time dealing with someone who will never be satisfied with any outcome. If they are unwilling to return the item for a refund, it means they are willing to keep the item, end of story.

Always try to be nice, but if the buyer insists on being rude or demanding or even threatening negative feedback, I don't negotiate. I am happy to work with reasonable people, but I have learned not to waste 90% of my time with 1% of people who will not be happy with any resolution.

Some buyers are satisfied to know their complaints have been heard and understood and will never return the item for a refund.

138

Part IV Selling
Chapter 17 - Shipping

You should be ready to ship the item even before the auction ends. Have the box and packing materials prepared and mark the box with the weight.

Pack it well and ship within a couple of days after receiving payment. If you can only ship one or two days per week, tell the buyer when their order will ship and remind them that you only ship on certain days. If you are using USPS as your shipper, you can print a shipping label and pay postage online. You can schedule pickups online and the postal carrier will pick up at your door.

PayPal has a feature that allows you to print a shipping label through their service. This is very handy and gives the buyer a record of the ship date and tracking number. You can buy postage and print the label through PayPal instead of going through the usps.com website. PayPal also offers UPS shipping.

PayPal only offers full protection to sellers if they ship to a Confirmed address. This is the address the buyer has verified by using a credit card. If the buyer has not confirmed their address, it will say Unconfirmed above the address of the buyer. Most sellers pay no attention to a verified or unverified address. This may work for inexpensive items, but you should only ship expensive items to the Confirmed address. If the buyer has not confirmed their address, ask them to do so before shipping for their own protection.

If anything makes you suspicious about the auction, make sure you only ship to the Confirmed address. If the seller ships to an Unconfirmed address and there is a problem with the buyer's funds, the transaction may be reversed.

DETERMINE YOUR SHIPPING COSTS

Always state the shipping costs in your auction. Bidders do not trust sellers who keep shipping costs secret. They are afraid secret shipping may be many times the expected cost, otherwise it would not be secret. You must list costs in the auction clearly and they must be reasonable.

You can weigh your item and use the USPS.com calculator to calculate shipping by Priority Mail. UPS.com and FedEx.com have their own online calculators if you plan to ship with those services. You can ship using the PayPal shipping system. All of these allow you to pay online and print a shipping label. If you do not have a scale and do not know the weight of the item, you can look at other auctions for the same item. See what they are charging for shipping. They should all be close to the same value. This will give you an idea of what it will cost. For small items this should work because most items can be shipped in flat rate boxes. Be careful when comparing shipping rates by other sellers. Some sellers may inflate shipping and use low opening bids or they may use high opening bids and shipping rates that are below their actual costs. If several sellers are offering the same shipping rate, then that should be a good value to use.

Make sure that your weight is for the item after it is boxed up and ready to ship. The box can add enough weight to push the package into the next weight class.

Never state in an auction that shipping will be calculated after the auction. This is a clear invitation for the seller to gouge the buyer and many potential bidders will pass over your auction if you do not have an honest shipping cost listed.

> *FedEx and UPS offer a buyer notification email option. If you use the FedEx or UPS websites to ship an item, include a description of what is being shipped. Nothing annoys a customer more than to receive an email saying "Your package has been shipped" with no indication about what the package contains. The buyer may not recognize your name as the sender and may have ordered several items. Make sure the buyer knows what item has been shipped if you use this auto notification system.*

Shipping costs do not have to be the actual cost of shipping. They should be MORE. Your costs are not limited to postage. You also have to package the item and you may have to buy a box. Boxes are not cheap. Even if you use free postal boxes, you will have to order them, store them, transport them to the post office, purchase packing material, buy tape, and take the time to package the item for shipping or hire someone to package the item. These all take money. It is perfectly acceptable to charge for shipping AND handling.

It is important to specify that you are charging for shipping & handling if your cost is above actual shipping costs. You should not say in the auction
Shipping is $12.00 if you are shipping an item that weighs one pound and can ship by Priority Mail for $5. You can say *Shipping & Handling $12.00* because this includes the actual shipping costs plus your packing and associated shipping costs. Make sure you always specify that you are charging for Shipping & Handling.

Suppose we were selling a small mp3 player that costs $5 to ship by Priority Mail in the USA. You can use a free postal box and salvaged bubble wrap to package it. Your real cost is $5 plus the gas and time to pack and take it to the post office. It would be very reasonable to charge $7.95 shipping. It would be absolutely unreasonable to charge $25 shipping.

There are many less than honest sellers on eBay selling small items for $10 then charging $40 shipping. Small and popular electronics like mp3 players and computer parts are often sold like this. This is simply a dishonest way of increasing the price.

☐		Samsung YP-T7 512 MB Digital Media MP3 Player BLUE		1	$0.99	$14.95	1d 45m
☐		512 MB MP3 Player w/Voice Recording by Nextar MA933A		=Buy It Now	$0.99 $3.50	$36.00	1d 02h 52m
☐		NEW 512MB i-Movie MP4/MP3/Pod/FM 512 MB Player Black		1	$0.99	$12.99	1d 02h 56m

Example of a seller charging a low price and excessive $36 shipping for a small item.

How do you determine shipping without knowing where the buyer will be? That is easy, you pick the worst case scenario. If you are in California, use the usps.com calculator to calculate shipping to New York 10001. If you are in New York, calculate shipping to California 93010. (These zip codes are just handy examples) Then add your handling costs to round it off. No matter what the destination, your shipping costs will be covered. Be sure to tell the buyer how you will be shipping. If the buyer pays $7 for shipping a small item then receives it in a first class envelope, they will be very upset. A buyer who pays $7 shipping has a reasonable expectation that their order will be shipped by Priority Mail. Make sure you state in the auction not only the cost, but the shipping methods.

For international shipping, I usually quote one price for Canada and another price for the 'rest of the world' which is based on shipping costs to Australia. Those should cover your cost to just about anywhere.

You will need to know the weight of your item. A bathroom scale is not the best method. If it is under weight by one pound, your package may be returned to you causing delivery delays and headaches. If it is a pound or more over, you may pay a lot extra in shipping costs unnecessarily. You can buy a postal scale, where else, on eBay. You will need a scale if you are a regular shipper. If you only ship occasionally and you are willing to stand in line at the post office, the clerk will weigh your package for you. You need to at least estimate the weight so you can quote shipping costs in the auction. You can always over-estimate it for the auction to make sure you are charging enough. Use the usps.com calculator to estimate the cost. Weighing items at home allows you to purchase postage at home and avoid standing in line at the post office. If you are estimating the weight because you do not have a scale, you will need to ship from the Post Office so they can weigh the package.

Customers today are accustomed to priority and overnight shipping. Priority Mail has changed people's expectations. You should always ship within two days of receiving payment and the customer expects to receive the item within the next 2 or 3 days. You can offer slower methods, but make sure the customer knows they are paying for ground shipping and they know how long it will take.

Low cost shipping can attract buyers. If shipping costs you $8.95 in postage, you can offer to ship for $5.00. This will make your auction more appealing when compared side by side with other sellers who are charging more for shipping. You can even offer free shipping if you are willing to roll the shipping costs into the final auction price. This can work well on expensive items that are small and can be shipped inexpensively. Offering low cost or free shipping gives bidders a reason to bid on your auction instead of another seller's auction. You can easily make up the price difference by attracting more bidders.

When buyers have a choice between an auction that lists shipping costs and one that does not, they will always choose to bid on the auction where they know the shipping costs. When a buyer has a choice between paying excessive shipping costs and low shipping costs, they will choose the lower shipping cost even if they pay more for the item.

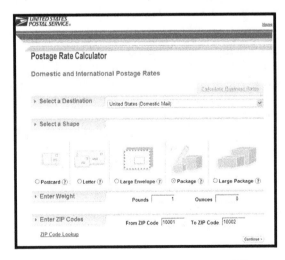

You can calculate postage and print pre-paid shipping labels using the US Postal Service Website at usps.com

You can also print postage for USPS and UPS from your PayPal account by clicking the SHIP button next to auction payments.

Buyers do not want to pay excessively high shipping costs for very inexpensive items. If you are offering a set of girl's hair berets for $2, buyers will not want to pay $6 shipping. This is a special case where you should offer First Class Mail shipping(with delivery confirmation) as standard shipping and then offer upgrade options for priority or overnight. I would have to question the point in selling an item for $2. *Is it really worth the trouble?*

Bidders don't think about shipping costs unless it is extremely high. As long as shipping is in a reasonable range for the size and weight of the item, bidders will not consider shipping when calculating their bid. If shipping is too high, bidders will adjust their bid. A music CD with $20 shipping will close lower no matter what the starting price is when compared to a CD with a $5 shipping price. Another CD with a $4 or $7 shipping cost will close at the same final bid level. Bidders will not consider any difference in the value as long as shipping is in a reasonable $4-$7 range. Reasonable shipping increases the number of bids. More bidding activity also means more potential for emotional bidders to run up the price. Keep your shipping rate reasonable.

Never list a shipping table in your auction. Don't make potential bidders do math. They do not like that. Use flat rate shipping and say what the shipping rate is. Don't throw a table at potential bidders and tell them to figure it out. I do not even like the eBay shipping calculator. Many sellers misuse the shipping calculator by putting in excessive weights which result in extremely high shipping quotes. I have passed over many auctions because the shipping calculator listed an outrageous shipping quote. State how much shipping is as a flat rate, no calculators, no tables, no 'after the auction I will tell you', no gimmicks, no math.

You can encourage buyers to use Buy-It-Now by offering free shipping. State in the first line of the description or subtitle "**Use Buy-It-Now and I will ship Free in the USA**". This can generate an instant sale. There is no reason to do this if the opening bid is close to the buy now price. Use this technique when you can set a Buy-It-Now price with a good profit margin that takes shipping into consideration.

What if you charge $10 for shipping and find out it actually costs $22?
You pay the shipping and weigh more carefully next time. It is never appropriate to contact a buyer and ask for more shipping money. The buyer already agreed to the posted price and shipping costs. There is no re-negotiation. Asking for more because the seller miscalculated shipping is wrong. The seller is at fault, not the buyer. Be more careful with the next auction and make sure the shipping quote is accurate.

Never make bidders contact you for shipping costs. Bidders hate having to wait for shipping costs. Put shipping costs in the shipping section of the auction for both US and international shipping. Buyers know the costs before bidding and they can checkout using eBay's checkout feature.

Shipping costs, shipping methods, and payment methods accepted are part of the auction listing, but they should also be summarized in the description.

> *I once bought three auctions from a seller. The seller said in his auction he would combine shipping. When I went to checkout, shipping was not combined. He did not setup the auction correctly. I estimated the shipping cost and adjusted the total amount paid. I took the cost of shipping for one item and added a couple of dollars for each additional item. The seller could have shipped all the items in one box by Priority Mail which is flat rate so the amount was fair. The seller responded and accused me of trying to scam him. He said shipping would cost an additional $2.50. He thought I was going to scam him for $2.50 when I paid over $75 for the three items? If he had setup his auction correctly and openly stated what shipping would be for additional items then I could have sent the amount he wanted. He lost a future customer because I immediately added him to my bad seller list. I do not buy from sellers like this. If I win an auction and the seller does not specify shipping, I complete the checkout and add what I think is appropriate shipping. Sellers rarely complain.*

NEVER HOLD SHIPMENTS

Never hold a shipment while waiting for PayPal to transfer money to your bank account. A transfer from PayPal to your bank account is between you and PayPal and has nothing to do with the buyer. This is a sure way to gain deserved negative feedback. A seller who does this is making the buyer wait for no reason. Making the buyer wait after they paid immediately is unfair and pointless. When the money is in your PayPal account, you have been paid and should ship. If the buyer pays by eCheck using PayPal, then you will receive a notice from PayPal saying the payment is not complete. You can hold shipping until the payment clears for an eCheck. Never make a buyer wait for PayPal to transfer money to your bank account. Dishonest sellers use this tactic to prevent a buyer complaint from reversing the payment. The dishonest seller is trying to side-step PayPal buyer protection.

UPGRADE

Always offer a shipping upgrade. Some buyers like to receive things fast and will pay for it. This is where you can pad the shipping costs for some extra profits. This takes you extra time and trouble which is perfectly acceptable to charge for. Let's look at our mp3 player again. Suppose your standard shipping is Priority Mail at $7.95, you could offer a FedEx overnight for $27.95. It may only cost your $15 to ship it by FedEx and you can drop your package in the FedEx drop box at the post office. The only additional trouble for you is filling out the FedEx shipping label online instead of the USPS label, but your customer is paying for this special service upgrade. Always give customers an opportunity to pay extra for extra services.

INSURANCE

I guarantee every package I sell through eBay. If the the package is lost, or damaged, I simply issue a refund or ship a replacement. I rarely bother requiring a return of damaged merchandise unless I distrust the buyer. I do not purchase postal or additional shipping insurance unless the item is expensive or the buyer requests insurance.

If you are shipping an expensive item then you should purchase additional insurance. A $1,000 diamond should ship by a major carrier with plenty of insurance. The cost of insurance should be built into the price and not an additional charge on expensive items. Do not gouge the customer for an extra $10 just to insure something that should be insured anyway.

Even if a buyer does not pay for insurance, the seller is still responsible for the item. The FTC, Federal Trade Commission, requires that a mail order item be delivered within 30 days of receiving payment. If a buyer's order is lost, the seller cannot tell them *'too bad, you didn't buy insurance'*. The seller is still legally responsible for delivery or a refund.

Don't require buyers to pay insurance. Make it part of the shipping costs. When insurance is built in, buyers do not feel they are being gouged, and they cannot opt out. It can be a sales tool just like free shipping. "Buy now and I will include free insurance"

You can self insure inexpensive items and offer the buyer an option to pay extra for postal or carrier insurance. You cannot charge extra for self insurance. Charging extra for self insurance is against state insurance laws. Many sellers offer 'Free Insurance' and pad out the shipping costs. A seller can ship 20 eBay auction items and increases shipping by $1.50 each, then if one of those is lost in the mail, the seller can easily issue a $20 refund without losing any money. They have already recovered the cost from other sales. This is how insurance works. The customer is happy that they are not being charged for something that was lost in the mail and they may re-order from the seller later. The seller has not filled out any long tedious forms for a refund or filed a claim. Self insuring is much easier for the seller of small inexpensive items. NEVER say you are self-insuring in the auction. You cannot charge for insurance if you are not registered in your state as an insurance company. You can replace lost or damaged orders as a matter of good customer service. Self insurance is not really insurance. It is the seller making a customer happy by doing the right thing. A smart seller will cover their costs by adjusting shipping charges so they are not actually charging for insurance. Just make sure you do not charge extra for self insurance.

> *Warning: You cannot say you are offering 'self insurance' in your auction. This is not legal. States have insurance laws which prohibit selling self insurance. You can self insure and offer additional postal or carrier insurance that is optional. If the customer pays extra for shipping insurance, you MUST purchase that insurance by law.*

> We will not be held liable for lost, stolen, damaged, or misdirected
> packages shipped without shipping insurance. We will gladly combine shipping.

Confused seller attempting to disclaim liability. When you go into the Dry Cleaners and you see a sign saying 'not responsible for loss or damage' it does not relieve them from responsibility of loss or damage. Responsibility is determined by state law or federal law for mailed packages.

Notification

Notify the customer when their item ships and give them the tracking number along with the shipper website so they can track it. This is very important, especially when the customer is paying extra for a special service. They may need the item before a trip or for a special project. Receiving it and tracking it may be more important to them than the actual cost of the item. Customers like to know their payment was received and their item is on the way as well as how long they should wait. Always email a confirmation with tracking information.

I saw an auction on eBay where an arcade collector offered a CD of over a thousand photos from a large European arcade collection. The cost was $99 plus $7 shipping. Quite expensive, but I was really interested so I bid and won. I sent my PayPal payment immediately. A week went by and I received nothing. The seller never confirmed payment or a shipping date by email either. At $7 I reasonably expected Priority Mail shipping and was becoming concerned. I emailed the seller. at his @aol.com address. He did not respond after two days. I emailed again. Two more days passed and no response and no CD. I was now very concerned about my money. I filed a PayPal complaint because the item was well past due and the seller would not respond to my emails. The seller did respond to the complaint by blasting PayPal for allowing a complaint to be filed and blaming everyone but himself for the problems. Two days later the CD did arrive with $0.77 first class postage. I cancelled the complaint. It turned out that the seller decided to wait a week before shipping and then cheaped out on the shipping method which took longer. If this seller had simply responded to my emails, I would have been glad to wait and he would not have had to deal with a PayPal complaint. If the seller had shipped in a reasonable time or by Priority Mail or emailed to let me know when the item would ship, he also would not have had a PayPal complaint filed against him.

COMBINED SHIPPING

Always offer combined shipping if you have multiple auctions. Buyers are very likely to buy more than one item from you if you will ship all items together for a discount. They may even buy a second item they were not planning to buy. If you are selling small items, it may be possible to ship them together for the same price. You may want to offer $7.95 for the first item and $2 for each additional item. This is easy to setup in eBay auctions. You should ask yourself if the $2 really matters. If you can offer a flat rate for all items then you are likely to receive higher bids and multiple sales. You may even increase your Buy-It-Now prices by $2 and offer free shipping on additional items. Whatever you decide for your shipping discount on multiple items, you should list it in the auction.

Your costs will vary depending on the size and weight of the items. You may not be able to combine shipping if your items are heavy or large. You should explain why you cannot combine shipping for large or bulky items in the auction, if that is the case.

TRACKING

Always ship by a trackable method. You should never ship anything without delivery confirmation or a tracking number. When you ship online by Priority Mail, it includes delivery confirmation. If there is any question about the shipment or if the buyer files a PayPal complaint, you must have this tracking number. Do not ship anything without a tracking number.

USPS does not offer true tracking. They only offer delivery confirmation. They are not reliable when it comes to scanning items. Sometimes items are not scanned when picked up and sometimes they are not scanned on delivery. Delivery is quite reliable and shipping costs are so cheap that I still prefer Priority Mail with delivery confirmation as my primary shipping method.

Tracking is a problem with international shipments. USPS does not offer tracking except for Global Express shipping. You can ship by other carriers that do offer tracking or take the chance. I generally ship international orders by USPS if the item is inexpensive or replaceable. I almost never have a problem as long as I ship to modern industrial countries.

POST OFFICE

If you are not familiar with shipping packages, I suggest taking your items to the post office and shipping them through the window clerk. After a few trips to the postal clerk, you will understand how to fill out the forms and how to ship the packages on your own.

Online shipping is the best option. You never have to wait in line and you can process packages anytime. You can even order free shipping supplies like Priority Mail boxes and customs forms through usps.com. I ship almost everything by USPS Priority Mail with delivery confirmation. The post office provides free envelopes and boxes and it looks very professional when it arrives.

Reporting a missing package to the post office usually results in a look of sorrow and confusion from the clerk, but sometimes they can find a package by delivery confirmation number if the package made it to the buyer's local post office. If the USPS delivery confirmation number does not show delivered after a week, I assume the package is lost. I then verify the buyers address and reship, or just issue a refund if the buyer says it has not arrived. Delivery Confirmation may sometimes show the package as undelivered even if the package was delivered. Delivery confirmation labels are not scanned at every delivery by the delivery person even though they are supposed to be scanned.

It is standard practice with 'The Big Shippers' to deny every claim based on poor customer packaging. By doing this, many claims simply go away. This is why it is important to package items well. Keep this in mind when you file a claim.

You should always use a computer printed shipping label. Any shipping website will allow you to print the label on your printer. Handwritten labels are unprofessional and they can result in lost packages. If you must handwrite, make sure it is legible. Not just legible, but easy to read by anyone, who speaks any language.

Shippers will provide free boxes for their premium services like Priority Mail, or 2nd Day Services. If you are in a tight or need a special box, you can purchase them at your local office supply, U-Haul, or UPS Store(Formerly Mailboxes Etc.)

Your choice of shipping carrier will depend on your item. If you have an expensive or irreplaceable item, you will ship by a carrier that offers true tracking like UPS or FedEx. If you can absorb an occasional misdirection or lost package, you can save some money by shipping USPS.

INTERNATIONAL SHIPPING

International shipping may sound frightening if you are not familiar with shipping items outside the USA. It is actually very easy especially for small packages. The usps.com website has details on all of the requirements and your local postal clerk can explain it to you. International Priority Mail is the best option for shipping small items. International shipping requires a simple customs form that lists the package contents and who it is being sent to.

EBay is not just in the USA. EBay is worldwide. International bidders can increase the final bid even if they are not the ultimate auction winners. You are most likely to ship to Canada, Australia, and Europe. Depending on what you are selling, your main countries may be different. Some items are popular in France and not popular in England for example. If you select International Shipping, your auction will also show up on the international eBay sites like eBay.com.uk eBay.ca eBay.de. Your highest potential bidder may never see your item if you do not offer international shipping.

Don't forget to specify your flat rate international shipping costs for international buyers if you are shipping internationally.

```
LC690692856US
```

United States Postal Service
Customs Declaration **CN 22**
May be opened officially   See Instructions on Reverse
Do not duplicate without USPS approval.

☐ Gift   ☒ Commercial sample
☐ Documents   ☐ Other

Quantity and detailed description of contents (1)	Weight (2) lb. oz.	Value (3) (US $)
Gold plated neck chain jewelry		45.00

For commercial items only
If known, HS tariff number (4) and country of origin of goods (5) | Total Weight (6) | Total Value (7) (US $)

I, the undersigned, whose name and address are given on the item, certify that the particulars given in this declaration are correct and that this item does not contain any dangerous article or articles prohibited by legislation or by postal or customs regulations.

Date and sender's signature (8)   1-1-2020

PS Form 2976, January 2004

Customs Declaration CN 22 — Sender's Declaration
I, the undersigned, whose name and address are given on the item, certify that the particulars given in this declaration are correct and that this item does not contain any dangerous article or articles prohibited by legislation or by postal or customs regulations. This copy will be retained at the post office for 30 days.

Sender's Name & Address

Senders Name
123 Main Street
Downtown CA 90001 USA

Addressee's Name & Address

Buyers Name
456 Main Street
BIGCITY BC V4C 6P5 CANADA

Date and sender's signature   1-1-2020

Detached from PS Form 2976, January 2004   **Post Office Copy**

Filled US Customs Form PS Form 2976 CN22 for small items. A minimum value of $1.00 is required. This form is generally for items less than 16 ounces and under $400 in value. For large items, or items over 16 ounces, or more expensive items, form 2976-A is used which is a white form. Both are available from the Post Office and the clerk will help you fill them out.

Your shipping software should take care of this form for you.

Include an invoice or printout of the auction that shows the final ending auction value. Some buyers may request a lower value on the customs declaration so they do not have to pay taxes on received shipments. If you short the value, you are responsible. If customs inspects the $20 laptop you are shipping and decide it is worth $800, you may find yourself with a fine or bigger legal trouble. List the honest sale price of the item.

If you do not put an invoice in the package, the package may be held by customs. If customs agents do not believe the listed value, they will hold the package and send a notice to the recipient requesting price confirmation. When the buyer contacts you, fax the invoice or auction printout to prove the value.

The customs description should be complete and accurate. General descriptions like "medicine", "clothing", or "food" will not be accepted by customs and may be returned or held for inspection. If you are sending a cook book, call it USED COOK BOOK WITH RECIPES not BOOK.

If you are sending a dog collar, don't call it a 'DOG ITEM'. That will trigger a customs inspection because it is not clear and looks strange. Keep the description short, but make it clear and complete.

Gift? Commercial Sample? Document?

If the recipient is not paying for the item, it is a gift. If they are paying for it then it is a Commercial Sample. If John in Minnesota buys an item as a gift for his sister in London, that is a gift because his sister is not paying for it. If the sister in London buys the item on eBay, it is not a gift.

Do not charge extra for a customs form or for 'international processing'. This puts potential bidders off. Pad out the international shipping rate by a couple of extra dollars if you hate filling out the forms, but don't list a separate charge for it. This makes buyers, international or not, feel they are being nickel and dimed. Pick one rate. Never split shipping costs into categories.

Shipping small international packages is simple and only requires the white or green customs forms. Green for small packages and white for larger packages. If you want to ship something really large, it requires more paperwork. The postal clerk at your local Post Office can show you how to fill out the forms.

ENVELOPES AND SIGNATURES

Requiring a signature can cause packages to be missed. Many people are not home during the day to sign for a package. If the buyer uses a mail box service, someone else will sign for the package so there is only proof of delivery for insurance purposes and no proof the recipient received the item. If you use signature confirmation, make sure the buyer knows to expect it. They may request shipping to an alternate address.

I frequently use USPS International Priority Flat Rate envelopes for shipments. I purchase bubble envelopes to use inside of the free cardboard envelopes. The bubble mailers add more protection. Some additional clear tape can hold it together. It is surprising how much you can fit in one of these envelopes when you need to.

Always double seal your USPS free shipping envelopes and boxes with clear packing tape. The peel and stick glue on USPS packaging is very poor and will release after a few hours if you do not use additional tape. Do not use masking tape. Masking tape is for masking and not sealing. It will release when the package heats up during shipping and the package will open. Do not use thin transparent tape. It is not strong enough and will break during handling. Purchase real packing tape which is clear and comes in large rolls.

I purchased a very rare arcade game from a seller in Canada. The game was Apollo 14 and was released in 1970, at the time of the Apollo 14 program. I was high bidder at $1500.00. I contacted North American Van Lines(NAVL) special high value shipping division, the Beltman Group beltmann.com. They quoted me a shipping price of $650 from Quebec to California. Before I could have such a large and expensive item shipped I also needed a customs broker. If you have an item shipped from another country to a port, you will often receive a call from a broker who will handle the customs forms and delivery. I had to setup a customs broker in advance therefore, I needed to hire a customs broker on my own. NAVL recommended a firm they use so I called them. After filling out some authorization forms and paying $300 in processing fees the delivery was on its way. If the game had been new or if it had not been originally manufactured in the USA, I would have also been charged customs duties. These would be charged directly to me from the US Customs Department. Fortunately this was an antique that was originally manufactured in the USA. In the end, this was a very expensive experience, but I now have an ultra rare game that I enjoy. The costs were $1500 for the game, $650 shipping, and $300 to the customs broker for a total of $2450.00. I was able to take care of everything by email and fax. It was not practical for me to pick-up the item myself, but I could have saved almost a thousand dollars if I could have driven across the border for a quick pick-up.

If a country does not accept International Priority Mail shipments, that is an indication that their mail service is unreliable. If you attempt to ship a package to a country that does not accept International Priority mail, the usps.com website will warn you. You should not ship expensive items to such places and you must accept that there is a risk that the buyer will never receive their order in countries that do not offer International Priority service if you ship by US Postal Mail. Ship by UPS or FedEx instead and make sure you have the tracking number.

PACKING

Always pack items well. Packages are handled very roughly by all of the packing services. Not only are they thrown, dropped, and tossed onto conveyor belts several feet away, they are jostled in trucks and planes for hours at a time. Pack well and you will avoid buyer complaints. Packing an item well will send a message to the buyer that you are a professional eBayer. This will make them less likely to complain if there is another small problem.

Newspaper is commonly used for packing, but I don't recommend it. It looks unprofessional and may not provide good protection for delicate items. Anything you can do to make your package look more professional will make the customer less likely to complain if there is a problem and more likely to be impressed by your service. If you have to buy packing supplies you can figure those into your shipping cost. It is easy to add $1 to the postage cost and $1 should more than cover the packaging peanuts, tape or other packing supplies.

Shipping peanuts are common. I save these when I receive a large package with them and re-use them. Many people do not like receiving these because they can make a mess.

Bubble wrap is one of the best shipping materials. It is easy to handle, available at local office supply stores, and does not make a mess. It can give a lot of protection to valuable items too. Use enough bubble wrap to hold the item still in the box. You should not hear it moving around when you shake the sealed box.

If you have a particularly fragile or valuable item, I suggest boxing it up with bubble wrap, then placing that box in a larger box and using Styrofoam peanuts. This will give the greatest protection and if the outside box is damaged, the item is still protected. You should also put the buyer's address and your return address on the inside box, just in case.

If you have an item that could be damaged by moisture, put it in a plastic bag. A good wrapping of bubble wrap and tape will protect from moisture unless the box is submerged.

> *I received an eBay purchase and the first thing I noticed was that it was stamped as Parcel Post. This is the cheapest shipping method available besides Media Mail. Neither of these should be used for eBay shipping. The first thing I thought was how cheap the seller was. I paid enough to cover Priority Mail shipping and to save two dollars the seller made me wait longer and shipped by a cheaper method. I had not even opened the box and I was thinking of negative feedback. You do not want your buyers to think this. Ship by Priority Mail.*

Priority Mail allows you to ship in a nice box provided by the post office, you ship fast, and the customer is happy. You may not be saving $2 using a cheaper shipping method. You may be buying an expensive headache.

> *I once received a package from UPS that contained junk. It spilled out on the floor in a pile of hacksaw blades, perfume bottles, empty boxes, popcorn snacks, and other lose parts. I had ordered a heavy roll of specialty paper in a long box. The box was mishandled and the roll came out. Instead of returning the box or notifying the company that shipped it, they took the contents from other people's packages that were also mishandled and tossed it into my box. This even included boxes with shipping labels on them for other people. These clearly were not meant for me. UPS filled my box up with other peoples stuff, taped it shut and delivered it to me. I guess they thought I wouldn't notice my $400 roll of paper was missing and my box was packed with junk. When I called the company I bought the paper from, they immediately knew what happened. Apparently this is not uncommon.*

Wow the Customer

Make the customer say '*Wow, cool, this seller knows what they are doing.*' when they open their package. This reduces returns and turns customers into repeat buyers. Use a new box, use bubble wrap, include a nice note. If your customer bought ten items from ten sellers and received all of them on the same day, which one does he remember? He remembers your package because it was the nicest one.

> *I bought a very expensive antique catalog worth $200. The seller put it in an envelope and put that in a Priority Mail box with no padding. It arrived safely, but when I opened the box and saw that my prized catalog was bouncing around, well let's say that I did not think well of the seller. I did not leave positive feedback either. This was a very expensive, irreplaceable item and they tossed it in a box with no protection. I purchased an antique art print from another seller. This seller found the perfect oversize flat box for it, carefully added foam padding around it and then put protective foam sheets around the rigid print to keep it from being scratched. He really did an excellent job of packing the item up. This is a seller I liked and I immediately added him to my Favorite Sellers list. I will be interested if he has any similar items on eBay.*

PART IV SELLING
CHAPTER 18 - END OF AUCTION

END OF YOUR FIRST AUCTION

I hope you will have a high bidder when your first auction ends. If you setup the auction correctly then the high bidder already knows the shipping cost and how to pay so they can use the eBay checkout system to send you a PayPal payment. It is all automatic and you will receive a PayPal notice saying the buyer has paid. Once you have logged into your PayPal account to verify the payment is complete, you should send the buyer a message either through eBay or by email saying you received the payment and when you will ship. You should also send the tracking number. If you use the PayPal shipping feature, the buyer will receive this information automatically. Buyers like to receive a response when they send payment. They want to know they will receive something for their money. If a buyer sends a payment and never hears from the seller, they may assume they have been scammed and act hastily. Sending a simple email with shipping date and estimated arrival time can save you many PayPal complaints or negative feedbacks.

You can easily track your sold items using the Sold section of your MyEBay page.

IS YOUR SALE FOR REAL?

Buyers are not the only victims of scammers. Sellers can also be targets. Take a look at your buyers closely. If they have zero feedback or low feedback then check any feedback history. Do they have a history of non-payment? Was their account registered the same day as the end of the auction? Has the buyer contacted you and asked to send payment, but requested that you ship to another address or country? These are all warning signs that the buyer is not legitimate.

> *Your winning bidder may be a fraudulent bidder if their account is new with zero feedback and it was registered the same day the bid was placed.*

If it looks fishy, do not ship the item until you are sure it is legitimate. Use eBay's feature to Request Contact Information for the buyer and call them to confirm. If the buyer's name or email name does not match the PayPal payment name/address, then do not ship. If it looks fishy then don't ship anything! Report the buyer to eBay and PayPal immediately. You do not have to ship if you think you are going to be defrauded. Refund the customers money and request payment by another means like money order. Then hold the item until payment clears.

Give buyers enough time to pay. Some buyers will send payment by money order which can take a week. It may take them a couple of days before they can buy a money order, then the postal time to reach you. The post office can delay or misdirect mail which will cause more delays. Returned postal mail can take weeks to months to be returned. A Priority Mail package sent to a wrong address may take a month or longer before it is returned to the sender.

A buyer may have to transfer money into their PayPal account to pay for the auction which can take a few days. Some buyers may not deal with auction purchases until the weekend. If you have not received payment after ten days, you should file the eBay Unpaid Item(non paying bidder) notice.

The buyer is likely not going to pay if they have not paid after ten days. There is no purpose in sending 'Please Mr. Buyer, you won my auction and agreed to pay, so please do so, please' messages. The buyer will pay or they will not. There is no magic phrase that will make them pay if they do not plan to honor their obligation.

Never threaten a buyer. There is no reason to threaten anyone. Threatening a deadbeat bidder with bad feedback or legal action will not make them pay and can make an honest bidder with a poor memory not want to pay. Making a deadbeat bidder mad can gain you negative feedback. You may be quite embarrassed if you send a threatening letter about non-payment and then receive a reply from the buyer's widow.

You do not have to say anything if you send the eBay Unpaid Item reminder. The eBay notice says it all. The automatic notice is a very nicely worded reminder to the buyer. This should only be used if the buyer has not paid ten days after the auction closed. It must be filed within 45 days after the auction close. If you are not ready to send an eBay payment reminder and the buyer has a long history of good feedback, send an invoice instead and congratulate the bidder on their win. This gives the bidder a reminder and shows them the total cost with shipping. If the buyer does not respond to the invoice within two days, they are likely not planning to pay. Go ahead and start the non paying bidder process with this reminder notice.

There is no reason to contact the buyer by telephone or to request their personal information from eBay if they are a non-paying bidder. They buyer knows they bid. They also know they were high bidder because they were notified by email. If they have not responded to the auction won notice and the official eBay payment reminder, there is no reason to continue pestering the buyer. They are a deadbeat bidder and nothing will change that.

By going ahead and registering their non-payment with eBay, you have started the process smoothly. Sending an email and waiting to see if they respond or pay is a waste of time and dangerous. If you send an email or two, the buyer will know they are going to be in trouble with eBay and may post negative feedback in retaliation when they receive the eBay notice. Go ahead and start the non paying bidder process with the official eBay Unpaid Item Notice. When the buyer receives this notice first, they will see it as a simple reminder. If it is the second or third notice they receive, they are more likely to attack the seller by leaving false negative feedback. You can file for a listing fee refund ten days after the non-paying bidder notice is sent. If the buyer has not sent payment by this time, they have no intention of paying. The buyer will not receive this notice, but when it is filed their account will be marked as a non paying bidder. Their account will be disabled if they receive three non-payment notices. This is frequently the reason you will see "Not A Registered User" note by the name of some bidders in feedback profiles.

You can find the procedure on eBay to file for your final value credit in the Help Section. First, file the official Unpaid Item notice 7-10 days after the auction. If the buyer has not paid ten days after that notice is filed, file for your final value fee credit. It is important to complete both of these steps for a non paying bidder. This is important not just to recover your money; it is more important to formally mark the non paying bidder's account so they will be removed from eBay after two more offences. You must file for the Final Value Credit to have a strike placed against the non paying bidder's account. You must wait ten days after the non paying bidder reminder is sent before filing a request for your Final Value fees, but you cannot wait more than 60 days after the end of the auction.

Feedback Profile

htndljwc (0) 🛡️ Not a registered user
Member since Apr-19-06 in China

Three Non-Paying Bidder Notices will cause a user to be kicked off of eBay.

Once a non-paying bidder has received three notices from three different sellers, his account will be automatically disabled.

If the buyer does not pay, remember to add him to your blocked bidders list so he cannot bid on future auctions.

If you file a non paying bidder complaint and then the buyer sends a check, wait until the check clears before shipping. I rarely receive bad checks, but when I do, they are usually late payments.

In MyEBay/Help, the non paying bidder section explains how to fill out a non paying bidder notice and recover your listing fees. Don't worry about any of this now. In my years on eBay I have only used this form a few times.

You can find a shortcut to the Non-Paying Bidder report link at http://portal.dont-bid-on-it.com

Buyer Backs Out

There may be times when a buyer wants to back out of a transaction. This rarely happens, but when it does, I am glad the buyer is honest enough to contact me and ask to be let out of their bidder contract. I almost always agree. You can file a mutual-withdrawal in the non paying bidder section of eBay which cancels the fees associated with the auction without penalizing the buyer or seller. Make sure you notify the buyer and let them know you plan to do this and that it will not affect their record. You can then re-auction the item or make a second chance offer to the next high bidder. I have had bidders contact me and say their child placed the bid or they bid in excitement before reading the complete listing. The reason does not matter. If they don't want the item I will tell them not to worry about the auction and consider it cancelled. This has only happened a few times in my years on eBay. Some sellers may find their buyers backing out for frivolous reasons. If the buyer's reason is *"I found it cheaper elsewhere"* That is not a valid reason and the person should be reported as a non paying bidder. A bid is a contract and a promise to pay, not an expression of interest in possibly purchasing.

Diffusing Fraudulent Bidders

Sometimes items do sell, but the high bidder never pays. If you find that your products receive a lot of false bids from people with no intention of paying, you can require immediate payment or limit bidders to those with PayPal accounts(PayPal Account Required). This is a setting in your auction options. This will keep away non paying bidders because only paid auctions will end and you never have to wait for the person to pay. If you are selling a popular video game, you may find children bid on your auction and never pay. Using the *Require Immediate Payment* option will stop such bids or at least require them to complete the transaction.

Second Chance Offers

Second chance offers are great when you have more than one product and you are using an auction format. Many times someone will find an auction and bid only to be outbid before the auction closes. This person may not find your next listing which can result in a lower price for the next auction or no sale at all. If you can offer this person a second chance to buy at their high bid, they may take it. This will result in higher sale prices and more sales. I almost always accept a second chance offer when I receive one from a seller. If I was interested in the item at my listed price, then I am still interested at that same price.

PART IV SELLING
CHAPTER 19 - RELISTING SECRETS

What if your item does not sell?

Sometimes items do not sell. Even popular items may not sell. The reason may be that it was in the wrong category, the opening bid price could be too high, or too low, maybe it was listed at the wrong time. Some people may think it is too expensive, others may think it is too cheap and it must be broken. It may have been listed at the same time twenty similar items were being auctioned. There may be something in the auction that makes potential bidders mistrust the seller. View your auction through a buyer's eyes and see what is wrong. Compare your auction to other similar auctions that closed with high bids. What is different between your auction and their auctions? Fix your auction.

If your item does not sell, you can relist it. The listing fee will be refunded if your item sells on the second listing. Only the Insertion Fee for the second listing is refunded. The fees for upgrades are not refunded. You must select the eBay relist option. If your item does not sell the second time, you still have to pay the listing fees. The insertion fee credit is automatic if your item sells the second time and you used the relist button from the original auction.

If you relist an item, whether it sold or not, all people who were watching the item in Watched Items on their MyEBay page will receive an automated email from eBay notifying them the item has been relisted. This can be a powerful marketing tool. Suppose you sold a popular 1950's toy space ship and see in your MyEBay section that twenty people were watching the auction. The next day you find a similar toy spaceship. You can post it normally to eBay as a new auction and hope those twenty people find your auction or you can go to your MyEBay page and select the option to relist this specific item. Then change the description/title/photos to the new product. All past watchers will receive a notice saying, '*The item you were watching, 1950's rocket ship, has been relisted*'. This is free advertising which is directed to those who are interested in your product.

The common advice for relisting an item is to lower your opening price. This is not always a good idea. If you are selling a collectable, try taking all new photos and relist at a higher price. Take more photos that show lots of details and post them all. Change the wording of the auction too. If your item did not open at $20, and you think it is worth $50, try relisting it at $75. Even if it does not sell, you can relist it again at $50 and the bidders who followed the auction will see the price drop from $75 to $50 which may make them feel like they can snap up a bargain.

There are several things you can do to improve the chances of selling on a relisting. Lowering the price is one, but raising it can also work as previously described. If the price is unrealistic then lower your opening price to a reasonable level. Check other auctions for similar items to see what their closing prices were.

Change the item category – You may have the item listed in what seems like the right category, but it may not be the best category. Some collectors watch certain categories for certain items. If your item is not in the category most of the collectors watch, they may not see it. See what category other similar items are listed under. You can relist your item under more than one category, but you have to pay as if you listed the item twice. Make sure your category is correct.

Check your photo – Your photo should be of good quality and show the item clearly. If you have a link to your own hosting service, make sure the picture is appearing in the auction. If it shows a broken image icon instead of the photo, check the url to your photo or switch to eBay's photo service. Take more photos and add those to the auction.

Check the description – Is the description complete? Did potential bidders ask questions that were not answered in the old description? Do similar auctions have information that is missing from your listing? Make sure your listing is complete and has all of the important information. Make sure your listing does not have spelling errors, grammar errors, and that it is not SHOUTING AT POTENTIAL BIDDERS! Add to your description if it is short or clean it up if it is too long.

Reserve price – This is a problem. You should not have a reserve price. Get rid of it. Start your opening bid at the minimum you are willing to accept instead.

Payment Options – Are you offering PayPal? You should. Payment options should be clearly stated in the auction description.

Shipping – Are you offering to ship to the USA only? If you are offering a small item that can be shipped internationally, offer international shipping. Is your shipping reasonable for the size and weight of the item? Make sure the shipping method and cost is clearly listed in the item description.

Return Policy – Is your return policy clearly listed? Do you need to improve it to build buyer confidence?

Auction Time – When was your auction listed? When did it end? Was there a major news event at the end time? Did it end on a holiday weekend? Maybe relisting with a different end time will attract more bidders. You can also wait a couple of weeks before re-listing. This will mean new eBay members have joined and old members have returned so you have a new pool of potential bidders.

CONCLUSION

There are sellers who have sold thousands of items and have large feedback ratings who do many of the things I say not to do. Imagine how many more sales and how many more satisfied customers they would have if they had been doing things right. High feedback numbers do not necessarily mean quality sales experience. I am sure you have learned a lot from this book if you are new to eBay or of you have been selling for years.

EBay is a fun place for buyers and sellers. You can find items you would never even know existed if it were not for eBay. You can make some extra pocket money or start a serious business for very little investment.

EBay is truly the world's marketplace and has changed the way people buy and sell.

I have given many examples of bad experiences I have had with eBay and PayPal, but these are not everyday occurrences. I have been using eBay and PayPal almost since they opened their doors. I have dealt with tens of thousands of customers as a seller and purchased thousands of items as a buyer. My positive experiences far outweigh my negative experiences with either company. I would not be recommending them so highly or advising anyone on how to gain the most from these services if I did not strongly believe they can benefit the lives of everyone.

There will always be scammers and dishonest sellers on eBay just as they are anywhere else money changes hands. There are some there right now. But, they will wash out with negative feedback soon and scammers always have to move to new accounts when their old accounts are exposed. Following the advice I have given will help you spot them and easily avoid these problem sellers and buyers.

If you do have a problem with another user you can find information on dealing with them in the eBay Security Center. The link is at the bottom of every eBay webpage. PayPal has its own security center which can help you recover funds. Read our **Scams and Scoundrels** book for more information on eBay scams and how to protect yourself. If you do not have this book, you can find it at ScamsAndScoundrels.com

WHAT NEXT?

If you have not already done so, setup your eBay and PayPal accounts. Start browsing eBay. I am sure you will find something you need or at least something that looks interesting.

After you have been on eBay a couple of months and have built up your feedback. Return and review this program again. You will understand so much more of it after you have a little eBay experience under your belt. You will re-discover tips you forgot about and many of the tips you did not notice before will suddenly make perfect sense now that you are familiar with the workings of eBay. This program is not just an introduction. It will be a valuable reference to both sellers and buyers.

I hope the advice I have given will not only save you from unfortunate experiences, but will help you to build a fun and profitable eBay business. You may only want to sell some extra items around the house. That is a great way to not only make extra cash, but you can contribute to the eBay community by helping others who need items you no longer want.

I still do business on eBay and with PayPal and I plan to continue doing so for a long time to come.

I am going to check my favorite categories on eBay right now to see if anything new has been listed I may want to bid on.

You should check your favorite categories too and enjoy the eBay experience.

NOW, you Can Bid On It!

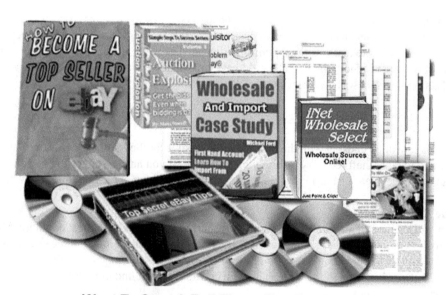

APPENDIX A
MORE INFORMATION

Take The Next Step!
You now know many tips and tricks that elude even the biggest sellers on eBay. Why stop there? Would you like to know how to make the transition from a part time seller to a full time eBay master seller? Then check out the eBay Mastery course. A complete course that explains how to create high profit products, how to import, how to sell at the highest profits, and more. Discover how you can become a full time eBay seller, go to http://Bonus.DontBidOnIt.com

Protect Yourself From Spoof Websites
Download the free My Little Mole toolbar from www.MyLittleMole.com
It will warn you if you visit a look-alike PayPal, eBay, or many thousands of other fake or scam websites. It also has some very useful search features.

Snipe Software
Only amateur bidders use proxy bidding. If you are tired of losing Snipe-To-Win with auction snipe software from www.snipe-to-win.com

Security, Credit Bureaus and More Information
Websites on the Internet change constantly. The website that was a great resource last week is gone today. The website that was the top information site last week is outpaced by a new website. We did not want to produce a book that would have links that were outdated by the time it went to press. This is why we always reference the

   http://portal.dont-bid-on-it.com page.

This webpage will be updated with the best websites. Visit it for the latest shortcuts to eBay pages, security and identity theft recovery information and more. If you have a suggestion that should be added to this page, please let us know. There is contact information at the bottom of the webpage.

Antique Arcade Games
I hope my discussion of antique arcade games has spurred at least some interest out there. Many people today have no idea these games even exist. There was a time before video games and it was a very rich culture of entertainment. If you like antiques, trains, old cars, or anything mechanical, you should check out some of these mechanical wonders. You can find more information and photos, at these websites
   www.classicarcadegrafix.com – Collector books on antique arcade games
   www.mechanicalarcade.com – Restoration information and photos of select antique games
   www.marvin3m.com/arcade/ – Excellent resource with history and photos of hundreds of games
and you can also check out the eBay category for Non-Video arcade games(this is where the antique games can be found when they show up)

   Home> Buy> Collectibles> Arcade, Jukeboxes & Pinball> Arcade> Machines> Non-Video

Is There Really A Secret System for Winning eBay Auctions?

Would you like to know a secret method to win auctions? How about a method that will also help you pay less. This is the method I, and thousands of others, have used to win countless auctions.

Bidding Excitement

I love the excitement of winning an auction. It's even better when I win at a bargain price. Is there a secret to winning auctions at the best price? Ohhh, you bet there is!

When I first started bidding on eBay® in 1998 it was a hit or miss experience. I would place a bid and hope for the best. I soon realized that I was being outbid more often than I was winning auctions. That is when my analytical nature came out. I started looking at bidding histories and noticed that frequently I would bid on an auction and someone else would bid several times in a row until they outbid me.

What was going on here? I was being outbid by people who were more interested in winning than in the item they were bidding on. I soon realized that if I placed a bid in the final few minutes, these people did not have a chance to run up the price and I had a better chance of winning. I later refined my technique to bid in the last minute and I was most successful when I bid in the final seconds. Later, I found out that this technique was used by others and it is actually quite common.

How To Win

The secret to winning eBay auctions is a technique called *Snipe Bidding*. Snipe bidding means placing a bid in the final seconds of an auction. By placing your bid in the final seconds of an auction, you avoid bidding wars, you keep your interest in the auction private, and you can snatch auctions away from inexperienced bidders who bid early and low.

Snipe bidding has both mathematical and psychological foundations. Even without

the analysis, cool headed, experienced bidders have known for a long time that it is highly effective. Mathematicians have shown that Snipe bidding works statistically. Researchers at Seoul National University in Korea analyzed over a quarter of a million auctions and confirmed that Snipe bidding gives the best chance of winning[1]. Bids placed early have less than a 50% chance of winning an auction.

Snipe bidding has strong psychological backing. Understanding the psychology of the average bidder will help the Snipe bidder win auctions. If the first person to place a bid makes a strong bid, it tends to attract those bidders who are looking for the thrill-bid. The thrill-bidders want to bid a few dollars more than the present bid to become the new high bidder. When they encounter a strong proxy bid that keeps automatically outbidding them, they will often continue bidding without regard for the item they are bidding on. They will run the price of the item up, satisfying their ego, but costing the auction winner extra money.

The majority of bidders do not think about what they are willing to pay and therefore do not bid their maximum. Instead, they bid either the minimum bid or an amount slightly above the minimum. They are afraid to bid 'too' much so they underbid. Snipe bidding takes advantage of this by placing your maximum Snipe bid at the last moment, without giving the amateur bidders time to reconsider their bid amount.

Bidding is a Vegas thrill for the amateur bidder. They become emotionally involved in the bidding process and may even bid more than the item is worth.

More experienced bidders know to avoid emotional bidding. The experienced bidder uses Snipe bidding to place their bid at the last moment. This prevents the unsure, amateur, or emotional bidder from running up the price. Let the amateurs put in their bids just above the minimum. The Snipe bidder will swoop in at the last second with a serious bid and take the auction at a better price than they would have received if they had bid against emotionally motivated bidders. Amateur bidders may think this is unfair, but they must realize that in the end, they were simply outbid by a higher bid.

Don't become trapped in a bidding war. Determine what you are willing to pay for an item before placing a bid. Make sure it is a price you will be happy with. The right price is what the item is worth to you. You can find a retail price from an Internet search for many items. On items that are not available anywhere else, like antiques, the price is whatever it is worth to you. Snipe bidding protects you from becoming involved in a bidding war or bidding emotionally instead of rationally.

Some thrill-bidders are not serious buyers. They have little or no intention of paying for an auction if they should win. These people can quickly run up bids against legitimate bidders. By placing bids during the final seconds of an auction, you take away the opportunity for these people to artificially inflate bid prices. This allows the Snipe bidder to frequently win auctions at bargain prices.

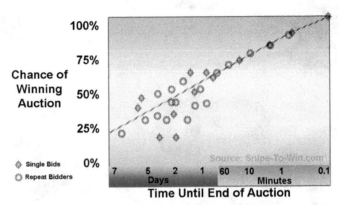

Early bids have less than a 50% chance of winning an auction

You can see from the chart how the probability of winning an auction increases for bids placed in the final seconds of the auction. Bids placed early in an auction have less than a 50% chance of winning. Chart from Snipe-To-Win.com. Graph information modified slightly to make meaning clearer. Graph data is derived from similar graphs in the paper "Bidding Process In Online Auctions And Winning Strategy: Rate Equation Approach" by I. Yang, and B. Kahng, Physical Review E 73, 067101 (2006)

Experienced Bidders Avoid Emotional Bidding

Are you still not convinced Snipe bidding works? Search eBay for closed auctions of a popular item. You will see that the winning bidder of one or more of these auctions placed the winning bid in the final seconds of the auction. Now, look at the bidding history of the winning bidder. A very high percent of their auctions have bids placed in the final seconds and, generally, the price is less than for similar auctions. Consistently winning bidders bid in the final moments because they know that Snipe bidding wins more auctions at better prices. It is an accepted fact among experienced bidders that Snipe bids win.

Snipe bidding is not a guarantee to win. The winner of the auction is not the last bidder, it is the highest bidder. The purpose of Snipe bidding is to avoid unnecessary bidding wars that run the price up for no reason. Snipe bidding increases your chance of winning and of winning at a lower price, but it is not a guarantee to win

every auction.

I can tell you from my own experience, I now win more auctions with Snipe bidding than I ever won by placing a bid and hoping for the best. If an auction does not have a Buy It Now option, I will use my Snipe-To-Win.com software to set a Snipe bid. I never use proxy bidding anymore.

The Benefits

Sniping is not just for bidders. Sellers who depend on emotional bidding may not like Snipe bidding, but most sellers love it. The ability to Snipe bid actually attracts more bidders. Many auctions close with no buyers, even when there are people watching the auction. This happens when potential bidders are not ready to place a bid, or want to check other auctions first and put off the bidding decision. Potential bidders may forget about the auction until it is over. This results in auctions with either no or very few bids.

Snipe bidders are seven times more likely to place a Snipe bid using software than they are to place a proxy bid through eBay. This is because Snipe bidders know they can cancel the bid at anytime before the end of the auction. Snipe bidders are much more comfortable placing bids when it is done on their terms. This brings in more bidders to an auction than it would otherwise have which benefits the seller. Snipe bidders tend to bid more often because placing a Snipe bid using software is so easy and they begin actively looking for bargains. The Snipe bidder can also calmly calculate the price they are willing to pay. They always know that if they win, they will receive what they consider a bargain price. In the end, Snipe bidding benefits both buyers and sellers.

Even The Playing Field

Bidding is like playing poker. You don't want to show your hand. Snipe bidding allows a bidder to maintain their privacy during an auction.

EBay is very much a community. There are specialized categories on eBay where everyone knows everyone else. The same people are watching for *doll head vases*, for example. If a well known collector wants to bid on an auction, they may not want everyone in the community knowing they are interested. Just knowing they are interested could make other bidders want to bid on the auction. *If Mr. Big wants it, then it must be something I want.* Snipe bidding allows those well know bidders to keep their hand secret until the last second.

Impulse bidders may see several existing bids in their category and feel a need to bid. They see everyone else bidding so they can't resist placing that bid even if it is for something they do not want. Snipe bids are not shown until the final seconds which keeps impulse bidders from gauging interest in the auction. They can no longer *'join the bidding crowd'*.

Snipe bidding has a way of evening the playing field for buyers. Various dishonest bidding techniques used by other bidders and sellers are easily thwarted by Snipe bidding.

Shill bidding no longer works against Snipe bidders. When a seller places fake bids using another eBay ID to run up the price, that is called shill bidding. If they overbid and become high bidder, they know the maximum proxy bid of the other bidders. They can then retract their bid and re-bid below that amount which artificially(and in violation of eBay rules) increases the price the high bidder will pay. Snipe bidding virtually eliminates the danger of shill bidding from less than honest sellers. The shill bidder cannot place a fake bid because they do not know what others will be bidding.

There have been instances where two bidders collude to fix an auction so they are guaranteed to win. One bidder places an unusually high bid, say $1000 on a

Snipe Bidding

Evens The

Playing Field

$500 item with an opening bid of $1. Then a second bidder working with him places a $1500 bid. No one else will bid on this auction. No one else CAN bid on this auction because they cannot bid less than the listed bids. Just before the auction ends, the second bidder cancels his bid leaving the first bidder at the opening price of $1. They have crushed any chance for other bidders to place a bid during the entire time of the auction so they are the only ones left. This is where Snipe bidding evens the playing field. This type of bidding activity can be obvious, especially to someone who is familiar with the auction item or category at eBay. A potential Snipe bidder sees a $500 item with a $1000 bid and immediately knows it is fishy. The bidder sets up his software to place a snipe bid for $300 in the final seconds of the auction. If the bogus bids are withdrawn, then the Snipe bidder's bid will be placed and he has a chance to win. He does not have to watch the auction daily or hope to catch it after the bogus bid is withdrawn. Snipe bidding makes this fake-bid scam ineffective keeping the eBay marketplace fair.

How do I snipe an auction?

When I started sniping I did it the old fashioned way. Set the alarm clock for 3 A.M., wait until the final seconds and click the Bid button. I would lose auctions because I would miss the end by seconds or my browser would be slow, or when I tried to place the bid I would receive the login screen. By the time I logged in, the auction was long over. Plus the process of bidding itself took several minutes. I had to load the auction, make sure I was logged in, watch the clock, refresh many times. I had to avoid being distracted and missing the auction end. It was also impractical to be at my computer when every auction ended. Manual Snipe bidding proved to be very inconvenient and unreliable. To this very day I regret losing these auctions. I can call out a list off auctions that I lost because I did not place my bid in time or forgot about the auction end. Placing a proxy in the final hours of an auction, before bed, invited unnecessary risk. While I slept, other bidders would bid up the price which resulted in me losing the auction or paying a lot more. That is when I realized there had to be a better way. The smart way to Snipe bid is using software.

Studies Prove...

Experienced bidders bid late. This is shown in various studies including Roth and Ockenfels* who studied bid timing for antiques and computers and compared the results and Wilcox* who monitored sales of tools and other items. Both of these studies find a clear link between late bidding and bidder experience. Experienced bidders bid late. Bidders who want to win bid in the final seconds of the auction.

*Ockenfels, Axel and Alvin E. Roth, "Late and Multiple Bidding in Second-Price Internet Auctions: Theory and Evidence Concerning Different Rules for Ending an Auction," Games and Economic Behavior, 55, 2006, 297-320 .and
Roth, Alvin E. and Axel Ockenfels, "Last-Minute Bidding and the Rules for Ending Second-Price Auctions: Evidence from eBay and Amazon Auctions on the Internet," American Economic Review, 92 (4), September 2002, 1093-1103
**Wilcox, R.T. 2000. Experts and amateurs: The role of experience in internet auctions. Marketing Letters, 11(4):363-374

There are two common methods for placing Snipe bids, not counting the manual method. One is to use a web based service that places the bid for you, and the other is to use software on your home computer.

Web Based Snipe Bidding

There are websites offering web based Snipe bidding. These systems require you to setup an account and charge a monthly fee to use their service. There are a number of disadvantages to using web based systems. Such services cannot offer privacy. You have to report to them what you are bidding on and what you are willing to pay. A central server is also a potential target for hackers. Hackers may attempt to access the login and credit card information for users, or they may begin a Denial of Service(DOS) attack which shuts the website down and prevents it from placing any bids. Placing many bids in a short time can also cause web based services problems. If a web based service knows it has 200 bids to place at 4:01 AM, it may start placing those bids early based on a formula that makes sure all of them are placed. There are numerous posts on the web from unhappy users complaining that their 15 second bids were placed minutes early or seconds late. Web based services may also restrict when bids can be cancelled. If you change your mind in the last few minutes before the auction ends, too bad, no cancellations.

I think this is a great business model. Sign up a bunch of people and charge them

a monthly fee... basically forever. As a bidder, I did not see why I should pay a monthly fee. Many bidders may not use the service for a month, but they are still charged if they use the service or not.

Software Snipe Bidding

Snipe software runs on your home computer and places the bids for you. Software Sniping is not only for people with high speed connections(DSL/Cable), but it will also work with dial-up Internet. I like software based systems the most because they offer privacy, security, and you have a desktop window that updates your auction status. You are alerted immediately if the bid exceeds your set Snipe bid before the auction ends. You do not have to check your email to find out you were outbid.

Software based systems can also offer many more features not available on web based services. Local software gives you instant alerts, real time monitoring of auctions, drag and drop auction watching, and customizable features.

You can calmly consider the price you want to pay and set it as your Snipe bid. Then you can forget about the auction. You will be notified when it closes if your bid was the high bid. Have you found a better bargain? Change your mind? Bought the same item locally? Negative feedback suddenly appears for the seller?

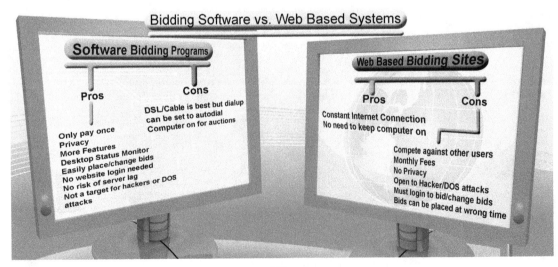

Bidding Software vs. Web Based Systems

Software Bidding Programs

Pros

Only pay once
Privacy
More Features
Desktop Status Monitor
Easily place/change bids
No website login needed
No risk of server lag
Not a target for hackers or DOS attacks

Cons

DSL/Cable is best but dialup can be set to autodial
Computer on for auctions

Web Based Bidding Sites

Pros

Constant Internet Connection
No need to keep computer on

Cons

Compete against other users
Monthly Fees
No Privacy
Open to Hacker/DOS attacks
Must login to bid/change bids
Bids can be placed at wrong time

If you used Snipe bidding software, you can cancel the bid with a couple of mouse clicks. Cancel your bid one second before the bid is placed if you choose.

Which method is best? It depends on your needs. If you are really serious and can't afford to lose an auction, use both. This gives you redundancy. Your local software will be the most reliable, but if your Internet connection hic-cups or your computer starts a virus scan that slows it down, the web based system may catch the auction for you. One danger is if the web based system places a bid too early. This may cause others to run up the bid and make you lose the auction or pay more than you would have if it were placed at the correct time.

Thrill of the Win

Using Snipe bidding still gives the thrill of the win. When I hear the auction won message and see the flashing WINNER! notice, I feel that winner's rush. Plus, I never have buyers remorse. My bid was set with a cool head and not emotionally motivated so I know the price I paid is one I am happy with. By avoiding the bidding frenzy I keep bids lower and I can buy more cool stuff.

What if you lose an auction? It happens. You can't be the high bidder every time. I think of it like this, if your bid is too low, you just saved yourself money for another auction. If you picked a good bid amount, with a calm head, an amount you are happy with, and you won, then you really are a winner.

Of course, you are welcomed to bid the old fashioned way, Go ahead, put in your proxy bid and hope for the best. But, be warned, if I am interested in the same item, I am going to Snipe that auction away from you. You have to Snipe-To-Win.

By Michael Ford
Entrepreneur, Author and Business Writer

Bibliography
1. NewScientist.com
http://www.newscientist.com/article.ns?id=dn9398

For more information on Snipe Bidding, or for a free trail version of Snipe software, visit www.Snipe-To-Win.com

Don't Bid On It Demonstration Video

See real demonstrations showing hot to use eBay and PayPal in the Don't Bid On It Video. It includes demonstrations which explain the bidding and price research process. You can see how to post an auction with all of the options explained. See how to setup your eBay and PayPal accounts if you have never done so before. The demonstration video also discusses some common selling mistakes and critiques several auctions while explaining how to post an auction that will maximize your profits.

Easily watch this video on your computer and follow along if you desire.

Reading about eBay is no substitute for having someone show you how it actually works. This video is like having your own eBay tutor in your home.

Get this video at http://www.Dont-Bid-On-It.com

CRIME On eBay
Learn how to protect yourself from scams on eBay

Learn to spot the most common scams and how to protect yourself. EBay and PayPal are excellent places to do business, but you also have to tread carefully in the sometimes dangerous Internet waters. New members of eBay offer prime opportunities for an experienced scammer. Don't give them the chance to take your money. Knowledge is power and the knowledge in *CRIMES On eBay* will help protect you and your family from criminals on and off of eBay.

This is a must read for anyone on eBay! Order your copy today at www.DontBidOnIt.com

www.ingramcontent.com/pod-product-compliance
Lightning Source LLC
Chambersburg PA
CBHW060138060326
40690CB00018B/3921